FOREIGN MILITARY SALES: PROCESS AND POLICY

HEARING

BEFORE THE

SUBCOMMITTEE ON TERRORISM, NONPROLIFERATION, AND TRADE

OF THE

COMMITTEE ON FOREIGN AFFAIRS
HOUSE OF REPRESENTATIVES

ONE HUNDRED FIFTEENTH CONGRESS

FIRST SESSION

JUNE 15, 2017

Serial No. 115–35

Printed for the use of the Committee on Foreign Affairs

Available via the World Wide Web: http://www.foreignaffairs.house.gov/ or
http://www.gpo.gov/fdsys/

U.S. GOVERNMENT PUBLISHING OFFICE

25–841PDF · WASHINGTON : 2017

COMMITTEE ON FOREIGN AFFAIRS

EDWARD R. ROYCE, California, *Chairman*

CHRISTOPHER H. SMITH, New Jersey
ILEANA ROS-LEHTINEN, Florida
DANA ROHRABACHER, California
STEVE CHABOT, Ohio
JOE WILSON, South Carolina
MICHAEL T. McCAUL, Texas
TED POE, Texas
DARRELL E. ISSA, California
TOM MARINO, Pennsylvania
JEFF DUNCAN, South Carolina
MO BROOKS, Alabama
PAUL COOK, California
SCOTT PERRY, Pennsylvania
RON DeSANTIS, Florida
MARK MEADOWS, North Carolina
TED S. YOHO, Florida
ADAM KINZINGER, Illinois
LEE M. ZELDIN, New York
DANIEL M. DONOVAN, JR., New York
F. JAMES SENSENBRENNER, JR.,
  Wisconsin
ANN WAGNER, Missouri
BRIAN J. MAST, Florida
FRANCIS ROONEY, Florida
BRIAN K. FITZPATRICK, Pennsylvania
THOMAS A. GARRETT, JR., Virginia

ELIOT L. ENGEL, New York
BRAD SHERMAN, California
GREGORY W. MEEKS, New York
ALBIO SIRES, New Jersey
GERALD E. CONNOLLY, Virginia
THEODORE E. DEUTCH, Florida
KAREN BASS, California
WILLIAM R. KEATING, Massachusetts
DAVID N. CICILLINE, Rhode Island
AMI BERA, California
LOIS FRANKEL, Florida
TULSI GABBARD, Hawaii
JOAQUIN CASTRO, Texas
ROBIN L. KELLY, Illinois
BRENDAN F. BOYLE, Pennsylvania
DINA TITUS, Nevada
NORMA J. TORRES, California
BRADLEY SCOTT SCHNEIDER, Illinois
THOMAS R. SUOZZI, New York
ADRIANO ESPAILLAT, New York
TED LIEU, California

AMY PORTER, *Chief of Staff*   THOMAS SHEEHY, *Staff Director*

JASON STEINBAUM, *Democratic Staff Director*

———

SUBCOMMITTEE ON TERRORISM, NONPROLIFERATION, AND TRADE

TED POE, Texas, *Chairman*

JOE WILSON, South Carolina
DARRELL E. ISSA, California
PAUL COOK, California
SCOTT PERRY, Pennsylvania
LEE M. ZELDIN, New York
BRIAN J. MAST, Florida
THOMAS A. GARRETT, JR., Virginia

WILLIAM R. KEATING, Massachusetts
LOIS FRANKEL, Florida
BRENDAN F. BOYLE, Pennsylvania
DINA TITUS, Nevada
NORMA J. TORRES, California
BRADLEY SCOTT SCHNEIDER, Illinois

CONTENTS

Page

WITNESSES

LETTERS, STATEMENTS, ETC., SUBMITTED FOR THE HEARING

APPENDIX

FOREIGN MILITARY SALES: PROCESS AND POLICY

THURSDAY, JUNE 15, 2017

House of Representatives,
Subcommittee on Terrorism, Nonproliferation, and Trade,
Committee on Foreign Affairs,
Washington, DC.

The subcommittee met, pursuant to notice, at 10:22 a.m., in room 2172, Rayburn House Office Building, Hon. Ted Poe (chairman of the subcommittee) presiding.

Mr. Poe. The subcommittee will come to order. Without objection, all members may have 5 days to submit statements, questions, extraneous materials, for the record, subject to the length limitation in the rules.

I have an opening statement. It is an excellent statement, but I am not going to give a statement at this time. I am going to file it in the record due to the time constraints that our two witnesses have today.

And so I will yield to the ranking member, Mr. Keating, from Massachusetts, for his opening statement if he wishes to give one.

[The prepared statement of Mr. Poe follows:]

Terrorism, Nonproliferation, and Trade Hearing
"Foreign Military Sales: Process and Policy"
June 15, 2017 10:00 a.m.
2172 Rayburn

CHAIRMAN TED POE OPENING REMARKS

The world we live in today is more dangerous than ever. Today, the threats we face are multiplied as not only traditional states but also violent non-state actors pose serious security challenges across the world. In this increased threat environment, the United States cannot be reasonably expected to fight or deter every challenge to peace and stability by itself.

To enable our friends abroad to defend themselves and maintain peace in their respective neighborhoods, the U.S. grants allies the opportunity to acquire vital equipment and training that will keep our mutual foes at bay. Foreign Military Sales are a key tool of United States foreign policy that provides needed security assistance to partners and allies around the globe.

For the last seventy years, the sale of American equipment to partner nations has formed the foundation of many U.S. security relationships. It is a key pillar of the U.S.-led order. The sale of American military equipment and services has a number of mutual benefits for both the U.S. and our allies.

American military technology and manufacturing are the best in the world. Thanks to our world-class industry, allies can better defend themselves rather than call on American servicemen and women to fight for them. The sale of U.S. hardware also bolsters the American industrial base. It creates thousands of high-paying, high-skill jobs here at home while reducing the cost of innovative technologies that keep the U.S. and its allies one step ahead of our enemies.

When our allies rely on U.S. equipment and technology, our armed forces can work better together, allowing vital inter-operability that saves lives and helps us win on the battlefield.

Earlier this year we sold the U.K. additional Hellfire missiles through the FMS process. Our closest ally needed more Hellfire missiles as their drones have been actively hunting ISIS killers in Syria and Iraq. The FMS process will allow the U.K. to strike back at the evil terrorists who committed acts of violence in London and Manchester and to reduce the burden on our own forces.

The FMS program is administered by the Defense Security Cooperation Agency and guided by the State Department. It ensures that friendly governments can purchase the items they require through a fair and legal process.

Importantly, Congress has oversight of this crucial and sensitive program. This provides an effective and transparent check on this key tool on our nation's foreign policy. When the administration notifies Congress of upcoming FMS sales, Congress can exercise its jurisdiction and weigh in on these important decisions. Foreign military sales provide other countries with deadly weapons of war. We must ensure that the countries we sell high-quality U.S. equipment share our interests and values.

Last year Congress rightly denied Pakistan the use of U.S. funds to purchase F-16s. Pakistan has long harbored, supported, and facilitated terrorist groups with American blood on their hands. Not only that, but Pakistan scrambled F-16s we had previously sold them in order to intercept American forces during the 2011 raid to kill Osama bin Laden. Pakistan intended to use American weapons against our forces on a mission to kill the most wanted terrorist on earth. Fortunately, Congress has a say about foreign military sales and blocked the sale of yet more F-16s to that state sponsor of terrorism.

Currently, the U.S. has negotiated billions in FMS deals with Saudi Arabia, a partner in the war against the Islamic State and other radical groups in the Middle East. Congress is examining these packages and will determine if they meet the interests of the American people.

In order to make more informed decisions regarding foreign military sales, we in Congress need to better understand the way the process works. There are no two better people to walk us through this vital process than the two witnesses we have with us today. I hope that they can also address current and future initiatives to reform the process. The FMS process can take a very long time, and that has frustrated both our customers and U.S. industry.

The DSCA has implemented some new efforts to streamline the process, but allies continue to express concerns. These concerns have led some of our friends to turn to foreign competitors to meet their needs more efficiently. These concerns need to be addressed. There is simply no substitute for U.S. technology and servicing. It is in our interest to ensure that our allies have the best. An FMS process that is efficient, transparent, and consistent with U.S. interests is crucial for both us and our allies.

And that's just the way it is.

Mr. KEATING. All right. Thank you, Mr. Chairman. I will just follow your lead. I know that our witnesses both have scheduling issues on the back end of this.

And I just want to share, the chairman, in my view, at the opening—frankly, not to keep mentioning this, but we can't keep it out of our minds, at the same time, that our prayers are with the victims of the shooting and the families that occurred yesterday, and all those that we serve with that suffered trauma from this. And a reminder across the whole country that every day, people are suffering from this kind of violence, and they are in our prayers as well.

So I will yield back, Mr. Chairman.

[The prepared statement of Mr. Keating follows:]

Terrorism, Nonproliferation, and Trade Hearing
"Foreign Military Sales: Process and Policy"
June 15, 2017 10:00 a.m.
2172 Rayburn

RANKING MEMBER OPENING REMARKS

Thank you, Chairman Poe, and thank you to the witnesses. You both have distinguished careers in government and the military and I look forward to learning from your expertise today on the topic of foreign military sales.

This is a very important issue because the military capabilities of our allies and friends is one of the many pieces of a comprehensive security strategy. The conflicts and threats we face cross borders; they take advantage of local, national, and international contexts; and they are enmeshed in geopolitics. The United States is <u>an important leader in providing military equipment to friendly countries</u> around the world to strengthen our own security and global security more broadly.

With this leadership, we have the opportunity to ensure that the military equipment being introduced into these conflict situations, is being used properly and in line with the legal and ethical standards that we and our allies stand for.

We have a quite extensive process for our foreign military sales, and I think process is important. We need boundaries to make sure that when we send our military equipment and technology into high security threat environments, that it is used appropriately and will not end up in the wrong hands.

However, this process is the product of regular scrutiny and consideration to make sure it is working in the most efficient and effective way.

I am therefore looking forward to hearing from the witnesses today on what is working and what is not, and what Congress can and should do to improve the process.

Most recently, an arms package for Saudi Arabia was signed and will go through our foreign military sales process. Saudi Arabia is playing an active role in the two most brutal conflicts unfolding in the Middle East right now and will continue to be a key player in the region.

Undoubtedly, it is important for the United States to play a meaningful role in bringing these conflicts to peaceful resolutions, and part of that role is related to our military sales to Saudi Arabia. I am not alone when I say that, while a critical partner in addressing many regional and global threats, some reports of Saudi military involvement in these conflicts warrant concern.

This underscores for me that it is critical that the United States continue to be engaged as a leader in setting high standards for the use of military equipment in accordance with international humanitarian law and the law of armed conflict. We are more secure if the United States is the one at the negotiating table when military equipment is changing hands.

So, I hope to hear from the witnesses today about how, first with the arms package for Saudi Arabia, and then going forward with future sales, we can be most effective with our foreign military sales process so that we – through these sales – can be sure to always *contribute* to promoting greater security and stability, and avoid at all costs ever exacerbating a conflict or the threat environment.

Thank you and I yield back.

____

Mr. POE. I thank the gentleman from Massachusetts for his comments. And to add a comment to what he has said, we do a lot of good things, I think, this subcommittee and other Foreign Affairs subcommittees. And those good things almost always are bipartisan. I mean, you can't get more bipartisan than Mr. Keating from Massachusetts kind of being somewhat left of center, and a Republican from Texas being a little right of center. We don't even speak the same language. But yet we are very bipartisan in here all the way through on both sides. And I want to make that statement because you don't hear that much here in Congress.

So, without objection, all witnesses' prepared statements will be made part of the record. I will ask that each witness please keep your presentation to no more than 5 minutes so the members here can ask you questions. I will introduce each witness and then give them time for their comments.

Ambassador Tina—tell me how to pronounce your name.

Ambassador KAIDANOW. Kaidanow.

Mr. POE. Ambassador Kaidanow is the Acting Assistant Secretary of State for the Bureau of Political-Military Affairs. In this position, the Ambassador manages the provision of more than $5 billion in international security assistance, bilateral transfers on commercial sales of U.S.-origin defense equipment, international security agreements, and implementation of the President's Export Control Reform Initiative.

Vice Admiral Joseph Rixey is the Director of the Defense Security Cooperation Agency. He previously served as the Deputy Assistant Secretary of the Navy for International Programs and Director for the Navy International Programs Office.

I also understand, Admiral Rixey, that you are going to retire. We object to that. And we still need you. But thank you for your long service in the United States Navy and serving the country.

Ambassador, we will start with you. You have 5 minutes for your comments.

STATEMENT OF THE HONORABLE TINA S. KAIDANOW, ACTING ASSISTANT SECRETARY, BUREAU OF POLITICAL-MILITARY AFFAIRS, U.S. DEPARTMENT OF STATE

Ambassador KAIDANOW. Thank you, sir.

And let me also express at the top, on behalf of the entire State Department and my colleagues—I am sure Admiral Rixey will also express the same—but our deep sympathy and condolences for those who were impacted by yesterday's shooting. I think that was really startling for all of us. And those of us who are so interactive at the State Department with our colleagues here on the Hill, we feel it very, very deeply. So, again, on behalf of the entire State Department, we wish them well, and we hope that they all will have a speedy recovery. So thank you.

Chairman Poe, Ranking Member Keating, committee members, I do want to begin today, first of all, by thanking the committee for holding this hearing and for joining us all here today.

It is right and it is proper that the Foreign Affairs Committee, and this subcommittee in particular, conduct oversight of U.S. arms transfer policy and procedures, because each of these, in our view, is fundamentally an act of foreign policy. In my testimony today, I will outline why this is the case, and I will walk through the process and the policy considerations by which the United States reaches a decision on when to and when not to offer or authorize the transfer of defense articles and services to a partner nation.

I am joined today, obviously, by Vice Admiral Joseph Rixey, director of the Defense Security Cooperation Agency, DSCA. And the partnership between the Departments of State and Defense, and particularly between my Bureau of Political-Military Affairs and DSCA, are stronger now than they ever have been, which is really key to our effective decision-making and policy implementation.

Admiral Rixey, as you said, will be retiring soon. And I want to take this opportunity to thank him most sincerely—and beg him, also, to stay—for the outstanding partnership that he and his team have provided to us.

In my written testimony for this committee, I provide an outline of how the arms transfer processes work in greater detail. But before you today, I would like to highlight three main points.

First, as I indicated at the outset, arms transfers constitute an element of foreign policy. We, therefore, take into account foreign policy considerations as we contemplate each arms transfer or sale, including, specifically, the appropriateness of the transfer in responding to U.S. and recipient security needs, the degree to which the transfer supports U.S. strategic foreign policy and defense interests through increased access and influence, allied burden sharing and interoperability, consistency with U.S. interests regarding regional stability, the degree of protection afforded by the recipient company to our sensitive technology, the risk that significant change in the political or security situation of the recipient country could lead to inappropriate end use or transfer, and the likelihood that the recipient would use the arms to commit human rights abuses or serious violations of international humanitarian law or retransfer the arms to those who would commit such abuses.

As a second key point, arms transfers support the U.S. defense industrial base and they reduce the cost of procurement for our own U.S. military. Purchases made through the foreign military sales, known as the FMS system, often can be combined with our Defense Department orders to reduce unit costs. Beyond this, the U.S. defense industry directly employs over 1.7 million people across our Nation. These individuals and the companies they work for represent a key part of American entrepreneurship and innovation, maintaining the United States as the world leader in the defense and aerospace sectors, and helping to ensure that our Armed Forces sustain their military edge.

In authorizing the transfer of defense articles or services, we take these considerations into account as well. For each export, we examine the effect of the proposed transfer on U.S. industry and defense industrial base, the risk of revealing system vulnerabilities and adversely affecting U.S. operational capabilities, and the availability of comparable systems from foreign suppliers.

A third key point: The arms transfer process works. The process is designed to review proposed sensitive transfers while balancing a very complex range of policy, industrial, and technological considerations. Even with all of that, the vast majority of sales move through the process quickly and efficiently. In some cases, certain considerations, for example relating to technology security, human rights, or regional balances of power, may slow or preclude the approval of a transfer. Such cases comprise a very, very small percentage of the overall caseload that we and our partners in DOD manage every day, but they tend to include some of the most high-profile cases.

I am often asked how we can "get to yes faster." As Admiral Rixey will describe, the most significant delays in the FMS system lie in the contracting and the production processes. But on those very rare occasions when a holdup involves the foreign policy part of this review, I will say this: Better a lengthy decision process that moves forward at the right time than a hasty process that puts sensitive technology in the wrong hands, ultimately undermining not only our security and foreign policy, but perhaps even our own industrial technological advantage.

Of course, there are always areas in which we can improve. We are working to complete the process of export control reform so that we shift jurisdiction over those defense articles and services that do not provide America with the specific technological advantage from the State Department to the Department of Commerce, where the process is a lot easier and faster. This will free up a significant portion of industry from unnecessary red tape and encourage innovation in our defense sector.

We are also working with Admiral Rixey to improve the FMS process, including through better educating and coordinating the entire defense security cooperation workforce across both the State Department and the Defense Department.

I will be happy to speak about these and any other initiatives before you today and to answer any questions that you may have about the arms transfer process. But just to conclude these brief remarks and to emphasize one more time, I am glad that this testimony is taking place, and specifically here in this context, because the fact that the House Foreign Affairs Committee has oversight of arms transfers speaks to the essential role that such transfers play in the construct of our foreign policy and the pursuit of our national security interests.

Your committee's continued interest and concern is a measure of the policy importance of these issues, and it tells both the American people and the rest of the world, frankly, that such transfers are not something the United States Government takes lightly. I look forward to taking your questions and also listening to any of your thoughts. Thank you.

[The prepared statement of Ambassador Kaidanow follows:]

OPENING STATEMENT TO THE SUBCOMMITTEE
ON TERRORISM, NONPROLIFERATION AND TRADE
COMMITTEE ON FOREIGN AFFAIRS
U.S. HOUSE OF REPRESENTATIVES

AMBASSADOR TINA S. KAIDANOW

JUNE 15, 2017

I would like to begin by thanking the Committee for holding this Hearing. It is right and proper that the Foreign Affairs Committee, and this Subcommittee in particular, conduct oversight of United States arms transfer policy and procedures, because each of these is fundamentally an act of foreign policy.

In my testimony today I will outline why this is the case, and walk through the process and policy considerations by which the United States reaches a decision on when to – and when not to – offer or authorize the transfer of defense articles and services to a partner nation.

I would like to start, however, by acknowledging that there are two witnesses before the Committee today. I am joined by Vice Admiral Joseph Rixey, Director of the Defense Security Cooperation Agency (DSCA). Arms transfers and other forms of security assistance are interagency efforts and, as you will see, the partnership between the Departments of State and Defense (DoD) – and particularly between my Bureau of Political-Military Affairs and DSCA – are stronger now than they have ever been, which is key to our effective decision-making and policy implementation. Admiral Rixey will be departing DSCA soon, and I want to take this opportunity to thank him for the outstanding partnership he and his team have facilitated between our respective organizations.

Before I provide a detailed explanation of how the arms transfer process works, I would like to highlight a few key points.

- Arms transfers are foreign policy. When we transfer a system or a capability to a foreign partner, we are affecting regional – or foreign internal – balances of power; we are sending a signal of support; and we are establishing or sustaining relationships that may last for generations and provide benefits for an extended period of time.
- Arms transfers also support the U.S. defense industrial base and DoD procurement. Purchases made through the foreign military sales (FMS) system often can be combined with DoD orders to reduce unit costs for our own military; beyond this, the U.S. defense

industry employs over 1.7 million people across our nation or about 3.5 million including indirect employment. These individuals and the companies they work for represent a key part of American entrepreneurship and innovation, maintaining the United States as the world leader in the defense and aerospace sectors and helping ensure our armed forces sustain their military edge.

- The arms sales process works. The process is designed to review complicated and sometimes contentious proposed transfers while balancing a wide range of policy and technological considerations. Despite the inherent complexity of the process, the vast majority of sales move through the process quickly and efficiently, and United States remains by far ahead of other nations in defense sales. In some cases, certain considerations – for instance relating to technology security, human rights, or regional balance of power – may slow or preclude the approval of a transfer. When this happens, it is a sign that the system is working to apply the careful consideration that is needed for such important transfers.

Overall Framework

Our approach to arms sales is driven by statute, regulations, and policy.

The key statutes through which we conduct arms transfers are the Foreign Assistance Act of 1961, as amended (FAA), and the Arms Export Control Act, as amended (AECA).

- Pursuant to section 622(c) of the FAA, the Secretary of State is responsible for the continuous supervision and general direction of military assistance and military education and training programs, including whether there shall be such assistance for a country. It is through this authority that the Department of State approves the transfer of Excess Defense Articles (EDA) under section 516 of the FAA. Such transfers must be consistent with section 502 of the FAA, which provides that defense articles and defense services may be furnished to a foreign government only for specific purposes, including internal security, legitimate self-defense, and to permit the recipient country to participate in regional or collective arrangements or measures consistent with the Charter of the United Nations.

- Section 1 of the AECA authorizes "sales by the United States Government to friendly countries having sufficient wealth to maintain and equip their own military forces at adequate strength, or to assume progressively larger shares of the costs thereof, without undue burden to their economies, in accordance with the restraints and control measures specified herein and in furtherance of the security objectives of the United States and of the purposes and principles of the United Nations Charter." Pursuant to section 2 of the AECA, "under the direction of the President, the Secretary of State (taking into account other United States activities abroad, such as military assistance, economic assistance, and food for peace program) shall be responsible for the continuous supervision and general direction of sales, leases, financing, cooperative projects, and exports under this Act, including, but not limited to, determining - (1) whether there will be a sale to or financing for a country and the amount thereof, (2) whether there will be a lease to a country; (3) whether there will be a cooperative project and the scope thereof; and (4) whether there will be delivery or other performance under the sale, lease, cooperative project, or export, to the end that sales, financing, leases, cooperative projects, and exports will be integrated with other United States activities and to the end that the foreign policy of the United States would be best served thereby." Section 4 of the AECA provides the purposes for which defense articles and defense services may be sold or leased, which include internal security and legitimate self-defense.

- The AECA also authorizes the President, in "furtherance of world peace and the security and foreign policy of the United States" to "control the import and the export of defense articles and defense services." The AECA requires that decisions on issuing export licenses for defense articles and defense services "take into account whether the export of an article would contribute to an arms race, aid in the development of weapons of mass destruction, support international terrorism, increase the possibility of outbreak or escalation of conflict, or prejudice the development of bilateral or multilateral arms control or nonproliferation agreements or other arrangements."

- There are also a number of restrictions that apply to arms transfers in the AECA, FAA, other statutes, or that apply through regulation or United Nations sanctions.

- We are further bound by our commitments to a number of international export control regimes, such as the Missile Technology Control Regime and the Wassenaar Arrangement.

Under the AECA, there are three main authorities through which the United States can provide defense articles or services to another country: government-to-government Foreign Military Sales (FMS); licensed exports of direct commercial sales (DCS); and the lease of defense articles. We are also authorized to provide EDA under the FAA and to approve third-party transfer requests under both the AECA and the FAA.

A variety of regulations apply to these programs. On the FMS side, government-to-government sales are implemented by the Department of Defense, and the Federal Acquisition Regulation and the Defense Federal Acquisition Regulation Supplement apply to all programs. Admiral Rixey will address this in more detail. On the DCS side, my Bureau manages the International Traffic in Arms Regulations (ITAR), which implements part of Section 38 of the AECA, authorizing the President to control the export, temporary import, and brokering of defense articles and defense services. Permanent imports of defense articles pursuant to section 38 of the

AECA are regulated by the Department of Justice's Bureau of Alcohol, Tobacco, Firearms and Explosives.

The ITAR includes the United States Munitions List (USML) – 21 broad categories into which defense articles and services may fall, ranging from small arms to naval vessels, fighter jets, and satellites. The export of articles and services enumerated on the USML are regulated by the Department of State, through the Directorate of Defense Trade Controls (DDTC).

While I will speak in greater detail about exports under the ITAR, it is important to note that the AECA requires every person who engages in the business of manufacturing, exporting, or importing defense articles or defense services to register with the Department of State. The ITAR implements this statutory requirement and clarifies that a "manufacturer who does not engage in exporting must nevertheless register." This requirement, according to the ITAR, "is primarily a means to provide the U.S. government with necessary information on who is involved in certain manufacturing and exporting activities."

Finally, regardless of whether an article or service is being transferred via FMS, DCS, Lease, EDA, or third-party transfer, we have a policy framework through which we review every arms transfer on a case-by-case basis. This is the Conventional Arms Transfer (CAT) Policy, a Presidential-level policy last updated in 2014. The CAT policy identifies 13 considerations we must examine in reviewing each sale or export:

- Appropriateness of the transfer in responding to legitimate U.S. and recipient security needs.
- Consistency with U.S. regional stability interests, especially when considering transfers involving power projection capability, anti-access and area denial capability, or introduction of a system that may foster increased tension or contribute to an arms race.
- The impact of the proposed transfer on U.S. capabilities and technological advantage, particularly in protecting sensitive software and hardware design, development, manufacturing, and integration knowledge.
- The degree of protection afforded by the recipient country to sensitive technology and potential for unauthorized third-party transfer, as well as in-country diversion to unauthorized uses.
- The risk of revealing system vulnerabilities and adversely affecting U.S. operational capabilities in the event of compromise.
- The risk that significant change in the political or security situation of the recipient country could lead to inappropriate end-use or transfer of defense articles.
- The degree to which the transfer supports U.S. strategic, foreign policy, and defense interests through increased access and influence, allied burden sharing, and interoperability.

- The human rights, democratization, counterterrorism, counter proliferation, and nonproliferation record of the recipient, and the potential for misuse of the export in question.
- The likelihood that the recipient would use the arms to commit human rights abuses or serious violations of international humanitarian law, retransfer the arms to those who would commit human rights abuses or serious violations of international humanitarian law, or identify the United States with human rights abuses or serious violations of international humanitarian law.
- The effect on U.S. industry and the defense industrial base, whether or not the transfer is approved.
- The availability of comparable systems from foreign suppliers.
- The ability of the recipient to field effectively, support, and appropriately employ the requested system in accordance with its intended end-use.
- The risk of adverse economic, political, or social effects within the recipient nation and the degree to which security needs can be addressed by other means.

I would like to stress that the CAT Policy is a framework, rather than an equation. Every transfer or export is considered on a case-by-case basis against all of the policy's criteria, in support of our foreign policy and national defense objectives.

Arms Export Processes

Let me now walk through the processes by which the United States may transfer or authorize the export of arms.

DCS

The first is Direct Commercial Sales. Generally in a DCS case, a foreign entity – be it a government, a corporation, or an individual – works directly with a partner in the U.S. defense industrial base to obtain equipment or services. Neither the U.S. military nor the U.S. government is directly involved in the sale or acquisition. If the articles or services in question constitute defense articles or defense services, as defined by the U.S. Munitions List and the ITAR, the State Department must authorize the transaction through a license or other form of approval. All such applications are reviewed under the CAT policy and other statutes or regulations as appropriate, and may include interagency review to ensure U.S. interests are properly protected. Depending on the nature of the transaction, the Department may convene an interagency working group to formulate policy recommendations on whether to grant the license or other form of approval. The composition of this group varies, but the main players include the Department and DoD. If the value of the license exceeds the levels identified in the AECA, the Department must notify the proposed license to Congress. Following State Department review, and, if required, the successful conclusion of Congressional notification, the Department may issue a license or otherwise approve the transaction.

FMS

The second major process is the FMS process. In FMS, a foreign country contracts with DoD to provide a defense article from stock or through a DoD purchase from the U.S. defense industry. In practice, this process constitutes several steps:

- Letter of Request (LOR) from the foreign partner. LORs can be vague, referencing simply an overall capability required, or they can lay out in detail a proposed procurement. LORs, which can be received via many channels, are processed by DSCA and turned into draft Letters of Offer and Acceptance (LOA), which provide far more detail, including cost. LOAs – once fully approved with the U S. government and accepted by the foreign government – ultimately constitute an agreement between the partner and the United States Government.

- The draft LOA is provided by DSCA to the State Department, where we review the case under the statutory, regulatory, and policy frameworks identified above. While processing times can vary depending on the circumstances of individual proposed sales, the State FMS review process is an efficient one. State reviews and adjudicates FMS sales offers on a daily basis, typically providing its assent in all but a small minority of cases.

- If the LOA is above monetary thresholds established in the AECA, we must notify the case to Congress before the sale can be approved.

- Once the Department has approved the sale, DSCA may offer the LOA to the partner country. Its signature on the LOA is contractually binding. DoD then implements the case.

Beyond being a government-to-government process, FMS differs from DCS in several key ways. The first is in economy-of-scale buying power. When buying through the U.S. military, a country may be able to leverage a purchase that a particular Military Service is already buying for its own use to get a cheaper unit price than they would otherwise. Alternatively, the country may be able to pool with the purchase of another country that is also working within the FMS process. This provides benefit to our Military Services and promotes our ability to build meaningful partner capacity overseas.

Another reason a country might choose to use FMS is that it may not have the capability or capacity within its government to effectively oversee the acquisition, so they are paying DoD to do it for them. DoD provides contracting support, requirements evaluation, logistics support, and works directly with the U.S. supplier. As the exporting party in a Foreign Military Sales case is the United States Government, FMS sales are exempt from the requirement for export licenses.

FMS provides what is called "the total package approach," which includes the aforementioned services as well as sustainment, technical support, training, and software/hardware updates. The total package approach may make an FMS purchase more appear more expensive on the front end, but the country is receiving much more than a defense article.

Finally, there are many countries that appreciate the transparency that comes with the U.S. system. For them, demonstrating to its public that the acquisition is free of corruption is a significant selling point of the FMS system.

There are advantages, as well, to purchasing through DCS. DCS is not subject to the DoD acquisition process, and thus allows another country to set its own standards for competitions and negotiate directly with the U.S. defense industry. DCS may at times be faster, and might also prove better for acquiring items not purchased by the U.S. military for its own needs.

As a general matter of policy, the U.S. government takes a "neutral" position on whether a customer selects FMS vs. DCS although there are some systems which, because of technological or policy sensitivity, we only sell via FMS. The important element is that partners buy American; the mechanism through which they do so is typically their choice.

Leases

Pursuant to section 61 of the AECA, the United States may lease defense articles in DoD stocks to an eligible foreign country or international organization if there is a determination that there are compelling foreign policy and national security reasons for providing such articles on a lease basis rather than a sales basis and are not needed for public use. The recipient country must also agree to pay in U.S. dollars all costs incurred by the United States, including replacement costs of articles if lost or destroyed while leased.

Each lease agreement must be for a fixed duration not exceeding five years. The President, however, may terminate the lease and require the return of the leased article at any time during the duration of the lease.

EDA

Under section 516 of the FAA, the United States may grant transfer or sell EDA to foreign governments. Once a U.S. Military Service deems an article to be excess to its requirements, such articles may be made available to eligible foreign countries. EDA defense articles are made available on an "as-is, where-is" basis, meaning that partners are required to pay for any refurbishment or transportation costs associated with the acquisition. EDA is an extremely effective program, as it allows the U.S. to provide valued defense articles to our partners while reducing storage and destruction costs for our Military Services.

Third Party Transfer and Retransfers/Reexports

Finally, partners may also acquire U.S.-origin defense articles via third-party transfer. If a partner who was the original purchaser of a U.S. defense article wishes to transfer – via sale, exchange, or grant –to a third party, the two parties must seek permission from the Department of State for such a transfer, in order to ensure it comports with U.S. foreign policy goals and technology transfer concerns. Similarly, under DCS, all retransfers, which entail transfer of a U.S. defense article within the same foreign country, or reexports, which involve transfer to a third country, require authorization from the Department of State.

Congressional Notification

Congress has a critical role to play in oversight of arms transfers, and I will briefly walk through that process for you.

As I described above, arms exports – DCS or FMS – above certain statutory thresholds identified in the AECA must be notified to Congress before the license can be approved, or the LOA issued.

This process commences each year with the annual "Javits" report and briefing to Congress on anticipated arms transfers in the coming year.

On the DCS side, as we receive license applications that reach the statutory notification thresholds, we submit them immediately to the Committee for "concurrent review." This gives the Committee time to review the cases while we conduct our own internal policy and regulatory reviews but does not prejudice the ultimate decision on whether or not to move forward with the case.

For nearly all DCS and FMS cases, once the Administration has made a decision to approve a license or an LOA above the statutory notification threshold, we provide a draft notification to the Committee under a process we call "tiered review."

This entails a Congressional review period during which the Committees can ask questions or raise concerns prior to the Department of State initiating formal notification. The purpose is to provide Congress the opportunity to raise concerns, and have these concerns addressed, in a confidential process with the Administration, so that our bilateral relationship with the country in question is protected during this process. If, during the Tiered Review period, the Committee raises significant concerns about a sale or license, we will typically extend the review period until we can resolve those concerns.

Following the conclusion of the Tiered Review process, we submit formal notifications to Congress. Depending on the country, statute allows Congress either 15 days (NATO +5+1 countries) or 30 days for Congress to object to a sale or license, which it must do through a concurrent Joint Resolution of Disapproval. If no such bill has passed within the Notification timeframe, we may offer the partner country the LOA or issue the export license.

I want to note how much we value this process of Congressional engagement. It is my experience that Congress brings a unique and fresh perspective to arms transfers, asking questions that help us sharpen our thinking and raising concerns that cut across different considerations, from protecting American jobs against the offshoring of manufacturing to pressing us to use arms sales to gain leverage on other aspects of a country's behavior or performance. I speak on behalf of both Admiral Rixey and myself – and our entire Departments – when I thank you for your continued oversight and engagement on this critical matter.

End-Use Monitoring and Compliance

I would like to conclude by discussing two essential aspects of U.S. arms transfers: end use monitoring and compliance.

End-Use Monitoring

End-use monitoring (EUM) refers to the steps we take to ensure that defense articles or services we have provided are used, secured, and accounted for, consistent with section 40(a) of the AECA, our license terms, and in accordance with our agreements with the foreign government or international organizations. Section 40A requires an EUM program for defense articles and defense services sold, leased, or exported under the AECA or the FAA that is designed to provide reasonable assurance that *i) the recipient is complying with the requirements imposed by the United States Government with respect to use, transfers, and security of defense articles and defense services; and ii) such articles and services are being used for the purposes for which they are provided."*

The U.S. government has three EUM programs for defense articles, technology, or services. EUM for USML articles and services exported via DCS is implemented via DDTC's Blue Lantern program. Blue Lantern's mission is to help ensure the security and integrity of U.S. defense trade. Blue Lantern helps prevent the diversion and unauthorized use of U.S. defense articles exported through DCS, combats gray arms trafficking, uncovers violations of the AECA, and builds confidence and cooperation among defense trade partners. Blue Lantern end-use monitoring includes pre-license, post-license, and post-shipment checks to verify the bona fides of foreign consignees and end-users, to confirm the legitimacy of proposed transactions, and to verify compliance with U.S. defense export rules and policies. Blue Lantern checks are typically conducted by U.S. embassy and consulate staff in over 100 countries every year. An unfavorable Blue Lantern determination may result in the denial or revocation of a license, entry on DDTC's Watch List, or, if there is evidence of possible criminal activity, referral to Homeland Security Investigations (HSI) or the FBI.

For FMS cases, EUM is conducted via DSCA's Golden Sentry program. The principal components of Golden Sentry's execution include obtaining pre-delivery end-user assurances from the recipient governments and international organizations regarding authorized end-use, re-transfer restrictions, and protection of U.S.-origin defense equipment. Routine and Enhanced end-use monitoring by security cooperation organizations assigned to U.S. embassies worldwide verify end-use, accountability, and security of defense articles and services. Compliance Assessment Visits performed by the EUM Division personnel are also central to the Golden Sentry program. Golden Sentry personnel from DSCA verify compliance with the end-use terms and conditions of sale and other transfer agreements.

Certain defense articles require specialized physical security and accounting. For these highly sensitive items, the Golden Sentry program conducts specialized Enhanced End Use Monitoring (EEUM) – a program that requires DoD security cooperation officers at our embassies to conduct EEUM through planned and coordinated visits to host nation installations, where they verify by serial number a 100 percent inventory of EEUM-designated items on an annual basis.

Compliance

There are two aspects of compliance I would like to touch on today. The first relates to foreign partner nations, and the second to foreign and U.S. commercial entities.

If our EUM checks determine that an unauthorized third party transfer has occurred, or that previously-transferred sensitive U.S. technology has been exploited, we may be required under section 3 of the AECA to make a report to Congress regarding the violation of our agreement with the foreign entity. There are a number of steps we may take to address such situations, up to and including the suspension of defense sales or exports to the country in question.

Corporations involved in the defense trade are responsible for ensuring their compliance with the ITAR. Most U.S. defense manufacturers have personnel dedicated to ensuring such compliance, and we work with hundreds of companies each year to ensure they are aware of the requirements and to address any compliance issues that may arise.

When significant lapses in compliance occur in the context of DCS transactions, the AECA authorizes a number of options for the U.S. government. These include pursuit of civil cases against companies or individuals who have violated the ITAR, potentially resulting in fines or export restrictions, as well as criminal penalties implemented by our law enforcement partners and the Department of Justice, if warranted.

Our civil cases most frequently result in administrative settlements, which often include Department oversight of the steps the company takes to address the cause of their lapse in compliance. The Department may waive or reduce a civil monetary penalty when companies agree to implement compliance-improvement measures.

In cases where criminal conduct has occurred, we assist our law enforcement partners, including the HSI and FBI, to support criminal proceedings by the Department of Justice.

Conclusion

..

We recognize the challenges associated with U.S. arms transfers. Across the interagency, we work day in and day out to ensure transfers are carefully considered, and approved or denied for the right reasons that promote American security and American interests.

Each delivery of U.S. defense articles and services sends a message to our friends and foes. It is an act of support and trust for our partners and allies. It provides them the capabilities to defend themselves and to support the security and stability of their region.

At the same time, defense transfers and exports provide significant benefits to the United States, not only in strengthening our partners and partnerships but also in terms of our own military procurement and the health of U.S. defense industrial base.

Most arms transfer decisions have a clear and swift path to approval, as we work expeditiously with DoD to support our partners and allies worldwide. Others will be more difficult, owing to the wide array of criteria I've described today. While we cannot avoid accounting for the complexities of these foreign policy decisions, we must also continue to move ahead to build the capacity of our partners in support of our national security interests.

We recognize that to slow or impede this work would be to open the door for other suppliers and actors. It would hamper our allies' efforts to work with us on common security issues. It would distance us from our partners. It would disadvantage the very industry on which we rely for our technological security capabilities and advantage. It would take away our voice in circumstances where it might matter the most.

We therefore transfer arms within the context of laws, regulation, and policy designed to ensure that our security policy reinforces our diplomacy and foreign policy. And we see results every day, from support for coalition operations against shared threats, to multinational training exercises, to the conversations that occur between American troops and foreign partners – partners who came here for training and left here as friends. We will remain judicious in using arms transfers as a tool of foreign policy, but we should never forget that our national security is in many ways dependent upon, and advanced as a result of, our security cooperation.

Thank you.

Mr. POE. Thank you, Ambassador.

Admiral Rixey, you have 5 minutes.

STATEMENT OF VICE ADMIRAL JOSEPH RIXEY, DIRECTOR, U.S. DEFENSE SECURITY COOPERATION AGENCY

Admiral RIXEY. Thank you, Chairman Poe, Ranking Member Keating, and members of the committee. And before I get started, in light of yesterday's events, I simply want to state thank you for serving.

I am pleased to be here today in my capacity as the director of the Defense Security Cooperation Agency, DSCA, to discuss the overall health of the foreign military sales, known as FMS. I am summarizing my written statement and ask that it be submitted for the record.

Mr. POE. Without objection.

Admiral RIXEY. Under the offices of the Under Secretary of Defense for Policy, DSCA leads the execution of the Security Cooperation programs, a wide range of activities enabling a full spectrum of capability the department seeks to provide its foreign partners. FMS is the government-to-government process through which the U.S. Government purchases defense articles, training, and services on behalf of foreign governments authorized in the Arms Export Control Act. FMS's longstanding Security Cooperation program that supports partner and regional security enhances military-to-military cooperation, enables interoperability, and develops and maintains international relationships. Through the FMS process, the U.S. Government determines whether or not the sale is of mutual benefit to us and the partner, whether the technology can and will be protected, and whether the transfer is consistent with U.S. conventional arms transfer policy.

The FMS system is actually a set of systems in which the Department of State, Department of Defense, and Congress play critical roles. The Department of Defense, in particular, executes a number of different processes, including the management of the FMS case life cycle, which is overseen by DSCA; technology transfer reviews overseen by the Defense Technology Security Administration; and the management of a defense acquisition and logistics systems overseen by the Office of the Under Secretary of Defense for Acquisition, Technology, and Logistics, and the military departments.

This process, or a version of it, also serves as well in the DOD Title 10 Building Partnership Capacity arena where the process of building a case, validating a requirement, and exercising our U.S.-acquisition system to deliver capability is modeled on the FMS system.

I want to say clearly that, overall, the system is performing very well. The United States continues to remain the provider of choice for our international partners with 1,700 new cases implemented in Fiscal Year 2016 alone. These new cases, combined with adjustments to existing programs, equated to more than $33 billion in sales last year. This included over $25 billion in cases funded by our partner nations' own funds and approximately $8 billion in cases funded by DOD's Title 10 program or Department of State's appropriations. Most FMS cases move through the process relatively quickly, but some may move more slowly as we engage in deliberate review to ensure that the necessary arms transfer criteria are met.

It should be noted that the validations required by the Arms Export Control Act, such as foreign policy or technology transfer reviews, occur regardless whether sales conducted via FMS or direct commercial sales. When foreign partners choose FMS, however, they are assured that their procurements are executed with the same level of confidence as ours, and they will be receiving a total package approach that includes associated capabilities such as training, logistics, and maintenance.

Though the system overall is performing well, DSCA is working with DOD and interagency partners to continually analyze the FMS process and target areas of improvement to keep the FMS system responsive to partner needs and agile to support foreign policy and national security objectives. Together with our stakeholders, we have developed and are implementing a robust set of initiatives captured in our 6-year plan, Vision 2020.

In addition, we are advancing key reforms directed by the Fiscal Year 2017 National Defense Authorization Act. Our focus is to improve the quality of the workforce through professionalism, to ensure the right quantity of the workforce is accomplishing our mission, and to build a more effective requirements prioritization system to be responsive to the global combatant commands while managing limited resources.

We have a continuous improvement culture and have identified these priorities to address the mandates of the NDAA to better enable the United States to remain the provider of choice to our foreign partners, providing them with the full spectrum of required capabilities to train for, maintain, and sustain the products they receive through the FMS program. We are also developing options to provide more transparency in the process as it occurs to our FMS customers. The transparency initiative was started to facilitate the improvement of the timelines and the quality in the execution of FMS, through greater transparency and communication, with regard to each step of the process.

As I have noted, DSCA plays a key role, but we are only one element of the broader U.S. Government system for FMS. My intent today is to comment specifically on DSCA's contribution to this mission both in terms of the programs we execute and the initiatives we are championing, and at the same time demonstrate the linkages and close coordination between us and the larger FMS enterprise.

Distinguished committee members, I want to thank you again for the opportunity to sit before you today, and I look forward to your questions.

[The prepared statement of Admiral Rixey follows:]

**OPENING STATEMENT TO THE SUBCOMMITTEE
ON TERRORISM, NONPROLIFERATION AND TRADE
COMMITTEE ON FOREIGN AFFAIRS
U.S. HOUSE OF REPRESENTATIVES
"FOREIGN MILITARY SALES: PROCESS AND POLICY"**

VICE ADMIRAL JOSEPH RIXEY

Director, Defense Security Cooperation Agency

15 June 2017

Thank you Chairman Poe, Ranking Member Keating, and Members of the subcommittee. I am pleased to be here today to share with you my thoughts on the overall health and well-being of the Foreign Military Sales (FMS) process – from my vantage point as the Director of the Defense Security Cooperation Agency (DSCA). The FMS system is burdened but not broken, and we've made important strides not only within the Department of Defense (DoD), but across the interagency, in mapping out and implementing – important initiatives that can further benefit the Security Cooperation mission area.

Context

Building partnerships, supporting allies, and protecting national interests are essential elements of U.S. foreign policy and national security. These activities require a careful balancing of short- and long-term considerations and a deliberate decision-making process to ensure our programs and strategies reflect our values and serve our interests.

FMS is the government-to-government process through which the U.S. Government purchases defense articles, training, and services on behalf of foreign governments. Authorized in the Arms Export Control Act (AECA) of 1976, as amended, FMS is a long-standing foreign policy and national security program that supports partner and regional security, enhances military-to-military cooperation, enables interoperability, and develops and maintains international relationships. FMS is a key Security Cooperation tool, enabling a full spectrum of capability the Department seeks to provide its foreign partners.

The FMS process begins with a discussion with partner nations to determine their requirements, referred to as the Pre-Letter of Request, or Pre-LOR, phase. That determination is laid out in the LOR which the partner nation submits to the U.S. Government. Upon receipt, the U.S. Government begins a process of interagency and, depending on whether the case crosses certain thresholds, Congressional consultation that can lead to a Letter of Offer and Acceptance, or LOA. The LOA is a contract-like agreement to be signed by both the foreign government and the U.S. Government. Fundamentally, through this process the U.S. Government determines whether or not the sale is of mutual benefit to us and the partner, whether the technology can and will be protected, and whether the transfer is consistent with the U.S. Conventional Arms Transfer Policy. This is a simplified characterization of the process -- and I'll provide more detail later -- but upon positive validation of national security interests, and subsequent signing of the LOA by the partner, an FMS case flows into the DoD procurement process beginning with the Department negotiating a contract on behalf of the partner nation or making requisitions from DoD stock.

I want to note that this FMS process – or a version of it – serves us well in the DoD Title 10 building partner capacity (BPC) arena. While the requirements are generated in a different way and the source of funds is not the partner nation but a Congressional Appropriation, the fundamental process of building a BPC 'case', validating a requirement, and exercising our U.S. acquisition system to deliver a capability, is modeled on our LOA process.

I want to say clearly that -- while I can understand where some of the concerns regarding the timeliness of the process come from, overall the system performs very well. Most FMS cases move through the process relatively quickly, but some may move more slowly as we engage in deliberate review to ensure that the necessary arms transfer criteria are met.

The United States continues to remain the provider of choice for our international partners, with 1,700 new cases implemented in Fiscal Year 2016. These new cases, combined with adjustments to existing programs, resulted in more than \$33 billion dollars in sales last year. This included over \$25 billion in cases funded by partner nations' own funds and approximately \$8 billion in cases funded by DoD's Title 10 programs or Department of State appropriations.

DSCA's Role

Under the authority and direction of the Under Secretary of Defense for Policy, DSCA is responsible for the execution and administration of all Security Cooperation programs and activities of the Department involving the provision of defense articles, military training, and other defense related services by grant, loan, cash sale, or lease. FMS is a Title 22 U.S. Code authority, and DSCA operates the program, in consultation and coordination with the Department of State, on the basis of authorities delegated from the President. DSCA:

- provides policy guidance, oversight and funding for the Defense Implementing Agencies that execute FMS and other Security Cooperation programs;
- manages foreign partner and U.S. Government funds used to finance the transfer of defense articles and services; and
- determines training requirements necessary for the Security Cooperation Workforce to carry out its FMS and Title 10 Security Cooperation responsibilities. This includes approximately 14,000 FMS program supported civilian, military and contractor personnel in the United States, as well as Security Cooperation Office personnel located in U.S. missions overseas.

It is important to note that by law the FMS process is conducted at no cost to the U.S. taxpayer. Each sale has an associated surcharge that collects funding from partner nations into the FMS Trust Fund Administrative Surcharge Account. DSCA provides funds from this account to the Military Departments and Defense Agencies over the entire life of FMS cases to execute the FMS process and deliver the equipment, services, and training to our international partners.

In addition to operating a three-year budget cycle to plan for the future use of these funds, DSCA conducts frequent assessments on the overall health of this account to ensure that we have sufficient funds to deliver the very significant and growing undelivered value of current FMS agreements.

<u>The Process and DoD's Role</u>

DoD executes FMS through delegated authorities, and subject to the authorities of the Department of State. Our transfers are subject to the requirements of the Arms Export Control Act and the U.S. Conventional Arms Transfer Policy (Presidential Policy Directive 27). Before we make any transfer we must validate:

- that the sale is of mutual benefit to the partner nation and the U.S. Government,
- that the partner is willing and able to protect the technology according to our requirements, and
- that the transfer is consistent with our foreign policy objectives.

The FMS system is actually a set of systems which primarily involves three organizations which play critical roles – the Department of State, the Department of Defense, and the Congress. The Departments of State and Defense have extensive interaction and engagement with Capitol Hill counterparts throughout the year to ensure that information is shared to support the timely and comprehensive review of notified cases.

Under the AECA, cases that meet specific monetary thresholds must be notified to the Speaker of the House of Representatives, the Chairman of the Committee on Foreign Affairs of the House, and the Chairman of the Committee on Foreign Relations of the Senate for a period of time during which an LOA may not be offered to the foreign partner. During this period, Congress may seek to prohibit the sale through the joint resolution process. The State Department reviews each case through application of the Conventional Arms Transfer Policy, and also considers industrial base concerns and U.S. warfighter needs. The Department of Defense, in particular, executes a number of different processes in support of FMS, including:

- Management of the FMS case lifecycle, overseen by DSCA,
- Technology transfer reviews, overseen by the Defense Technology Security Administration (DTSA), to validate that our critical technologies will be protected, and
- Management of the defense acquisition and logistics systems, which are overseen by the Office of the Under Secretary of Defense for Acquisition, Technology and Logistics and

the Military Departments as they oversee the procurement of defense articles for the partner nation.

Criticism of the alleged slow approval timelines in the FMS program is largely associated with a few high-profile cases that have been the focus of the media and Congressional attention. I believe this criticism – while understandable, depending on where you sit in this process – is actually misplaced. In almost all instances, the FMS process is acting as designed in considering foreign policy, technology transfer, and industrial base concerns. These delays are natural outcomes of the validations required by the Arms Export Control Act, rather than a negative reflection on the performance of the FMS program itself. It should be noted that the validations required by the Arms Export Control Act -- such as foreign policy or technology transfer reviews -- occur regardless of whether a sale is conducted via FMS or Direct Commercial Sales (DCS). When foreign partners choose FMS, however, they are assured that their procurements are executed with the same level of confidence as ours and they will be receiving a total package approach that includes associated capabilities such as training, logistics, and maintenance.

Also, the Fiscal Year 2017 National Defense Authorization Act (NDAA) builds upon our work and empowers our efforts. Specifically, it:

- consolidates policy oversight and resource allocation within the Office of the Secretary of Defense and it consolidates execution and administration of Title 10 Security Cooperation programs within DSCA,
- requires DoD to provide a consolidated budget justification and establish an assessment, monitoring and evaluation framework to allow a more rigorous, data driven assessment of program effectiveness, and
- mandates DoD to establish a Security Cooperation workforce development program to ensure the approximately 14,000 Security Cooperation professionals all over the world have the appropriate training, education and experience to execute the mission.

Excess Defense Articles

The Defense Security Cooperation Agency is also responsible for administering the Excess Defense Articles (EDA) program. Working under the authorities of the Foreign Assistance Act of 1961 and the Arms Export Control Act, defense articles declared as excess by the Military Departments can be granted or sold to foreign governments or international organizations in support of U.S. national security and foreign policy objectives.

The Military Departments determine what is or is not excess. Equipment which has been transferred from the Military Departments to the Defense Logistics Agency, Disposition Services, is also available for transfer through the EDA program if an eligible foreign government makes known its requirements for the equipment.

The Department of Defense is authorized by law to transfer Excess Defense Articles to foreign governments under the following authorities:

- Section 516 of the Foreign Assistance Act (FAA) of 1961, as amended, authorizes grant transfers of lethal and non-lethal EDA to countries for which receipt of such articles was justified to Congress for the fiscal year in which the transfer is authorized. Among other factors, these transfers must consider the impact on the national technology and industrial base to sell new or used articles.
- EDA may also be sold to foreign countries under the normal FMS system authorized by the Arms Export Control Act (AECA). When EDA is sold, the price is a percentage of the original acquisition value, based on age and condition, and ranges from 5% to 50% of the original acquisition cost.

Initiatives

DSCA is working with DoD and interagency partners to continuously analyze the FMS process and target areas for improvement to keep the FMS system responsive to partner needs and agile to support foreign policy and national security objectives. We have a continuous improvement culture and have identified interagency initiatives to better enable the United States to remain the provider of choice for our foreign partners -- providing them the full spectrum of required capabilities to train for, maintain, and sustain the products they receive through the FMS program. The FMS process itself – the activities ranging from a partner submitting a Letter of Request through case closure – has been the subject of multiple assessments, process improvements, and Lean Six Sigma projects. Currently, we have efforts underway to improve the FMS process, founded initially in DSCA's strategic plan, Vision 2020, that address improvements to FMS process partnership, FMS process improvements, FMS process enablers, and integrating Title 10 transactions into the FMS work stream. In particular, efforts focus on activities in five distinct process areas in the FMS system: partner nation actions, the FMS case lifecycle, technology transfer, foreign policy review and oversight, and acquisition.

We are developing options to provide more transparency of the process, as it occurs, to the FMS customer. The Transparency Initiative was started to facilitate the improvement of timeliness and quality in the execution of FMS through greater transparency and communication with regard to pre-LOR, case development, and contracting processes.

DSCA just published a Transparency Handbook that lays out milestones and tools to improve the timeliness and quality in the execution of FMS. Specifically, it provides guidance to:

- Structure effective information exchanges,
- Encourage productive dialogue,
- Align partner needs with those systems and services that the United States has available, and
- Our ability to openly communicate with our partners across the continuum of FMS activities will foster better understanding as we work to achieve common goals going forward.

Another important focus of our attention has been contracting for FMS. DSCA has been working with the Office of the Under Secretary of Defense for Acquisition, Technology and Logistics on improving the responsiveness and effectiveness of contracting for FMS. The FMS program uses the same contracting and procurement system used by our Department of Defense. Foreign Military Sales are subject to the Federal Acquisition Regulation including the Defense Federal Acquisition Regulation Supplement, which are in place to ensure that the U.S. Government gets the best value for taxpayer money. We look to provide the same value for our partners. Our greatest challenge in the area of contracting is manpower, both ensuring there are sufficient billets in place to support both FMS and domestic contracting requirements and to ensure that there are trained and certified professionals available to fill the contracting officer billets.

Conclusion

As I've noted, DSCA plays a key role – but we are only one element of the broader U.S. Government system for FMS. In addition to other elements of the Department of Defense, the Department of State and other interagency stakeholders, as well as the U.S. Congress, play important roles. My intent today was to comment specifically on DSCA's contribution to this important mission – both in terms of the programs we execute and the initiatives we are championing – and at the same time demonstrate the linkages and close coordination between us and the larger FMS enterprise. Distinguished subcommittee members, I want to thank you again for the opportunity to sit before you today, and I look forward to your questions.

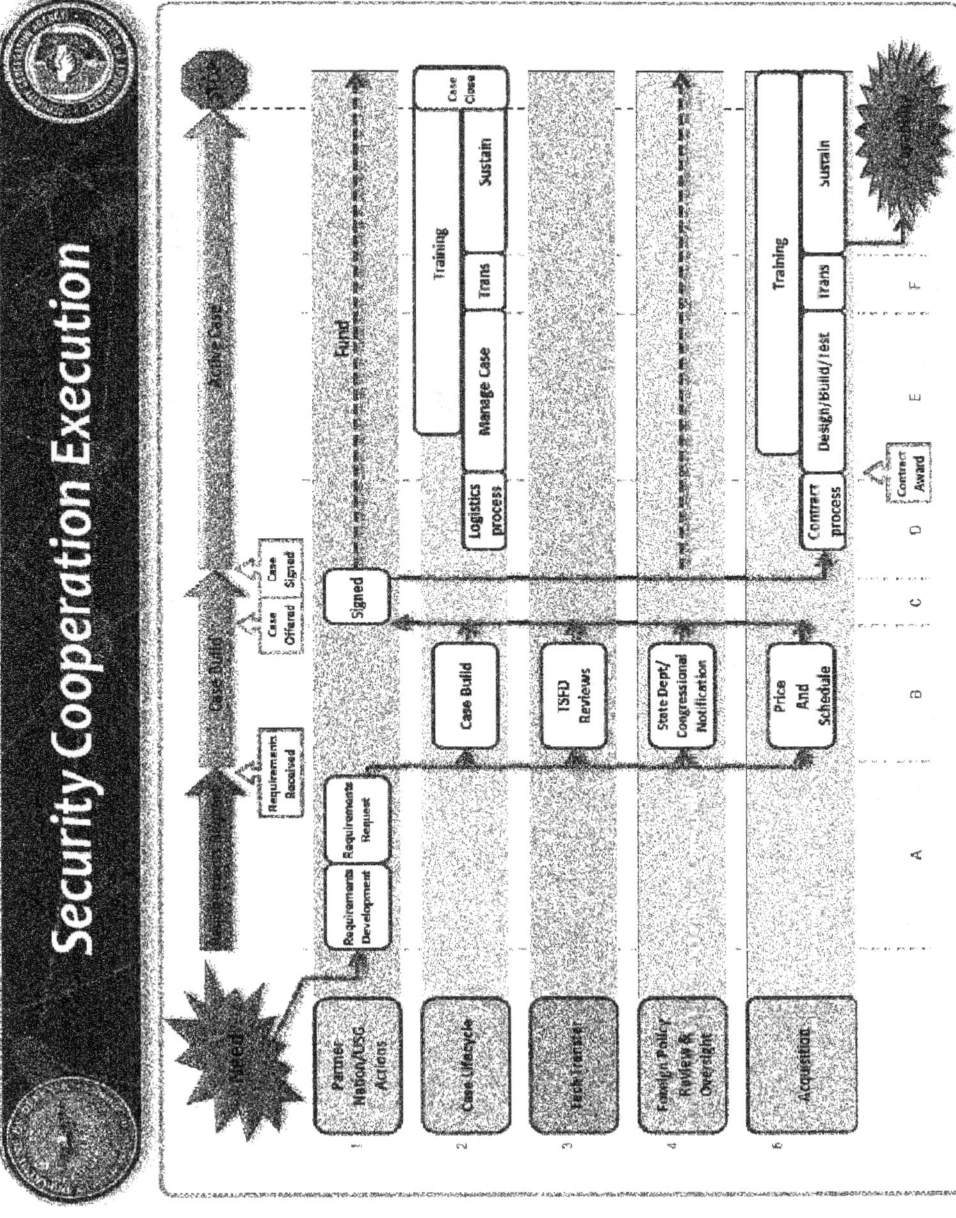

Security Cooperation Execution
Need
Active Case
Case Build
Requirements Received
Case Offered
Case Signed
STOP
Requirements Development
Requirements Request
Signed
Fund
Case Build
TSFD Reviews
State Dept/ Congressional Notification
Price And Schedule
Logistics process
Manage Case
Training
Trans
Sustain
Case Close
Contract process
Design/Build/Test
Training
Trans
Sustain
Contract Award
1 Partner Nation/USG Actions
2 Case Lifecycle
3 Tech Transfer
4 Foreign Policy Review & Oversight
5 Acquisition
A   B   C   D   E   F

Full-Spectrum Capability

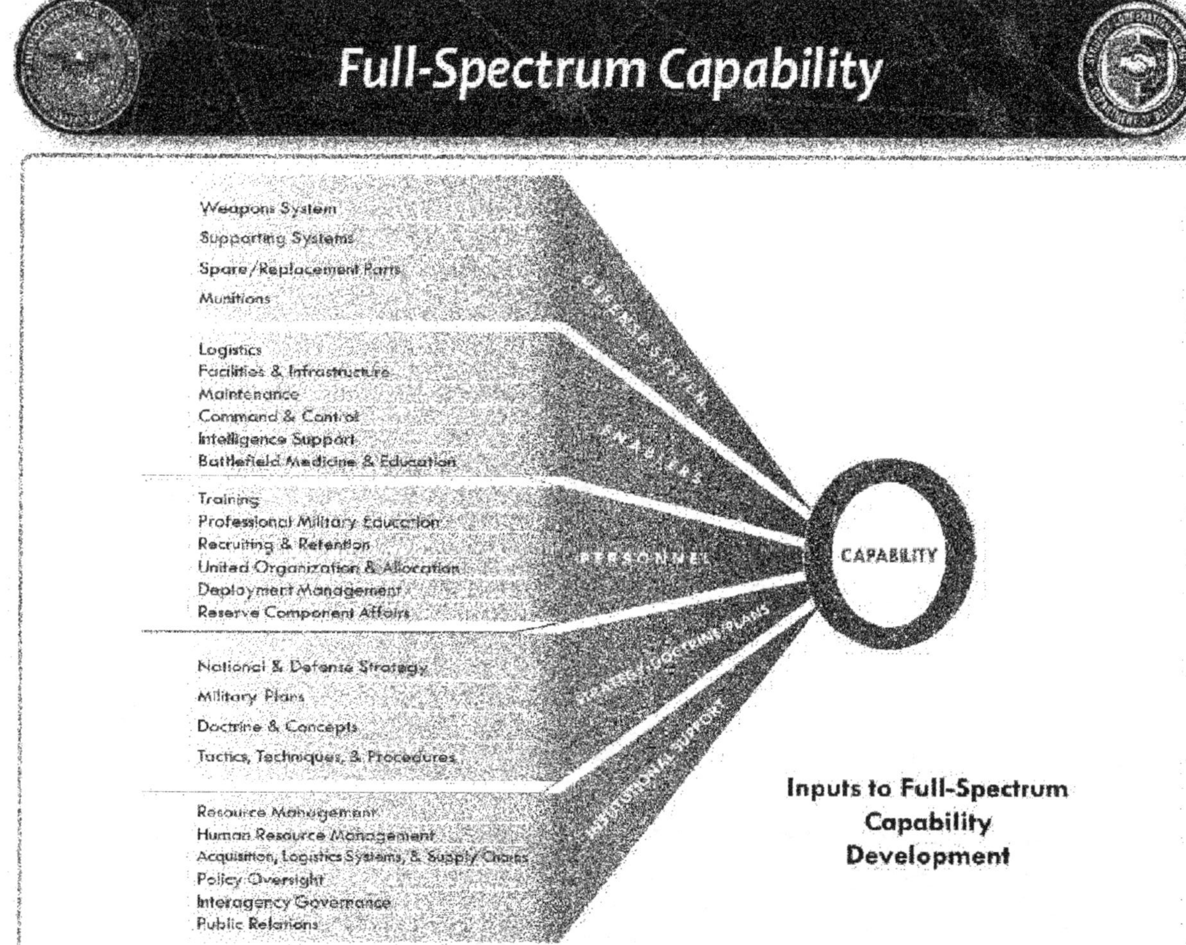

Mr. POE. Thank you, Admiral.

The Chair is going to recognize members in the order that they appeared. And I will reserve my questions till last.

So I will recognize the—without objection, I will recognize the gentleman from Florida, Mr. Mast, for 5 minutes of questions.

Mr. MAST. Thank you, Chairman.

Thank you, Ambassador and Admiral, for your time and your testimony. I want to get into a couple of quick questions on the process for FMS, as I am sure you are well aware that is what a lot of people want to talk about.

Can you outline for me a little bit just how the process can be made a little bit more streamlined when we are talking about just one U.S. competitor that is, you know, in there? Is there a place that that can be streamlined when there is just one U.S. contractor competing?

Admiral RIXEY. Well, first of all, in my submitted statement, I have two slides. The one is a Gantt chart. It really is a graphical depiction of the Arms Export Control Act.

Mr. POE. Is your microphone on, Admiral?

Admiral RIXEY. What is that?

Mr. POE. Microphone.

Admiral RIXEY. I am sorry. I submitted two slides with my statement. The first is a graphical representation of the Arms Export Control Act. It is really nothing more than a Gantt chart, critical path. There is a grid on it so that if we ever discuss FMS systems or FMS programs, we can be very specific as to where this program resides and how a case is particularly managing and going through a system.

The second slide that I provided you is the full-spectrum capability slide. At times throughout this testimony, I will be referring back to those slides to explain the process in a little better way.

As far as if a country requests a FMS case that goes sole sourced, we will honor that request. And so we will process that through the service acquisition community that will execute that case. I think that is your question. If it is requested by a partner, we will honor that sole-source commitment.

Mr. MAST. So you don't see a place where we are getting in the way there?

Admiral RIXEY. No, not at all.

Mr. MAST. Can you outline for me a little bit, you know, what would be the biggest concerns when you are looking to determine whether something is an inappropriate sale? What would be some of the examples? Or can you give me some specific examples of when you have identified that—you know, you are denying a sale because you thought it was inappropriate? Help me understand that process.

Admiral RIXEY. So, again, on that Gantt chart, you will see that it is a graphical representation of the Arms Export Control Act. There are three deliberate conversations that we have to have. It is based on the Arms Export Control Act and, actually, PPD-27. PPD-27—Presidential Policy Decision—has 13 considerations that we must make before we make a sale. I have thinned that down to three.

The first is, is it of mutual benefit? The first conversation we have is is it of mutual benefit. So we usually ask that question of our combatant commanders and the country team themselves.

The second deliberate conversation that we have is the technology. Will the technology be protected? Will they preserve it or will they have the agreements in place so that they will protect it?

And, third, the third deliberate conversation is foreign policy. For example, human rights or adherence to international norms.

So those are the three conversations we have. COCOM on mutual benefit in our industry—I am sorry—our country team in the Embassy, the DTSA under Beth McCormick, who leads that particular tech transfer and tech security foreign disclosure review, and then, of course, we work with State in terms of a foreign policy review.

Mr. MAST. And maybe this follow-on will go more to State. Maybe it will stick with you, Admiral, but——

Admiral RIXEY. Sure.

Mr. MAST [continuing]. How much are you consulting with other intelligence agencies when you are making these determinations as a part of that decision-making process?

Admiral RIXEY. The whole interagency process is engaged when we go through that deliberate conversation.

Mr. MAST. Okay. You have answered all my questions. I appreciate it. It gave me a much better picture of what you are doing there. Thank you.

I yield back.

Mr. POE. I thank the gentleman from Florida.

I recognize the ranking member of the committee, Mr. Keating, from Massachusetts.

Mr. KEATING. Thank you, Mr. Chairman.

Thank you for your testimony. I couldn't agree more with both of the witnesses in their opening statements that this is indeed a major foreign policy decision. Compared to some of the other policy decisions we make as a country, this can indeed have longer lasting consequences in many instances and have just as many intended and unintended results. So I agree wholeheartedly that these decisions can't be made in a vacuum. And you really did a great job laying out the procedure. So I am going to just put out two questions. And I know it will take up more of the time. But I like to give witnesses the ability, between both of you, to answer it.

And the first one is more specific, the Saudi commitments that were made. Now, if you can just articulate what some of the new commitments are and how they are different from the prior promises that were, frankly, reneged upon by the king to our country and, indeed, how they might entail changes in how they deal with civilian casualties, and maybe giving more assurances to coalition partners, follow those same policies and commitments as their coalition partners.

And then the second one, if you could, is the fact that—I said it is not done in a vacuum. What about our competitors, the other countries that are, you know, selling weapons to countries? You know, we know Russia, China, France, and I think interoperability. You laid all the reasons out why we should be where we are. But if you want to comment on the concerns you might have about how they do this business.

So those are the two issues, the Saudi commitments and just your own personal comments on how the other countries pursue this, and some of the concerns you have about the way they go about this as well.

Ambassador KAIDANOW. Thank you, Congressman. I think we had an opportunity, happily, earlier this week to brief some of you on this set of issues related to Saudi Arabia. So I got into a little bit more detail there than perhaps I can even here. But I will say this. We clearly believe that there is an interest in providing Saudi Arabia, but also some of the other countries in the Gulf, with what they need in order to carry out what we believe is both in our interests and theirs, and that is to counter some very serious threats posed by Iran and some other salient threats that we see in the Gulf region.

The President went not that long ago, obviously. We concluded with the Saudis—and the admiral can speak to this in greater detail even than I can—a large package of arms sales. The rationale behind that, in most instances is, in fact, to bolster the Saudi capabilities to do the kinds of things we have asked them to do. The buckets, if you will, or the elements of that package, are largely in maritime security, for example, border security, the kinds of things that, arguably, they really do need, and they need to improve by way of capability in order to push back on the threats that they have.

It is a large package, obviously. It will have other impacts that we can speak about. But, you know, the concerns that people feel about Saudi and the Saudi-led coalition's performance in Yemen are real. We share some of those concerns. We have shared that with the Saudi Government over time, and they have given us commitments that now, actually, I think have been in the public domain, but a number of commitments that we consider to be serious and credible, all of which are important. For example, adherence to the laws of armed conflict, vetting of targets. I mean——

Mr. KEATING. Yeah. We were also assured in personal meetings from the foreign minister of those changes as well. So I hate to interrupt. We are running out of time.

Ambassador KAIDANOW. No, please.

Mr. KEATING. But if either of you want to comment on the second question. You know, what are your concerns about the way some of these other countries do their business, you know, in terms of our own security here and the way they do it? I suspect they don't do it in as thoughtful a way as our process. But if you could take a little time—Mr. Chairman—to just do that, to enlighten us on what the other countries are doing.

Ambassador KAIDANOW. We obviously have those concerns, sir. And I think we try very hard to both monitor and also, then, to hold accountable the countries that violate those understandings. We belong to a number of different nonproliferation regimes. Missile Control Technology Regime, for example, is one of those. The idea is, again, to try and hold them to certain standards, and when they are not holding to those standards, hold them accountable.

I will say that, again, the American weapons systems remain the weapons systems of choice all over the world. We want to keep it that way. That is why we are trying to balance the technology security aspect of what we do against the ability of our defense industry, and the companies to do their business overseas, and to be as effective as they can be in as wide an array of countries——

Mr. KEATING. Yeah. And I think the interoperability issue is clearly an issue too because——

Ambassador KAIDANOW. Yeah.

Mr. KEATING [continuing]. Once they get these sales, and we don't, the tendency will be other sales will follow that, and these countries will have undue influences——

Ambassador KAIDANOW. That is right.

Mr. KEATING [continuing]. On areas we don't want them to have.

Ambassador KAIDANOW. Precisely.

Mr. KEATING. All right. Well, thank you.

I yield back, Mr. Chair.

Mr. POE. I thank the gentleman from Massachusetts.

The Chair recognizes the gentleman from California, Mr. Rohrabacher, for his questions.

Mr. ROHRABACHER. Thank you very much, Mr. Chairman.

Let me ask some specific questions about maybe some specific deals or policies. Egypt had a policy in terms of our sales of weapons to Egypt. It used to be where they would spend—they would put 20 percent down on a piece of military equipment, and then every year after that they would pay 20 percent. So after 5 years, they would pay for it, but they would be able to use that weapon system in the meantime. Egypt, as most of us know, on the front lines of the battle against radical Islamic terrorism, they are, themselves, targets. And I would say that if Egypt falls to a radical regime, the entire Middle East will fall.

Now, have we resumed the policy that we had before, instead of—I understand somewhere along the line, a few years ago, it became cash on the barrelhead. You have got to pay for that weapons system, all of it, on delivery. Which, of course, here we have someone on the front lines, the actual point of the spear of helping us fight radical Islam, and we are changing our policies to make it more difficult for them to have a weapons system. Has that been reversed yet or is that policy still in place?

Admiral RIXEY. Well, I think what you are referring to is cash flow finance.

Mr. ROHRABACHER. Yes.

Admiral RIXEY. But that is an appropriated account under foreign military finance. So it is not national funds from Egypt. So it is the State fund that we would provide to Egypt. We used to allow them cash flow finance, which means if we had $1.3 billion coming in a particular year, they could initiate a procurement of significant size because we knew the 1.3 was going to come next year and the following year. So they would have 3 to 4, 5 years of buying power.

Mr. ROHRABACHER. Right.

Admiral RIXEY. That was removed. So now that we are just—we will just take—we will not execute a case until the cash is there as financed, or cash on the barrelhead, as you said. That policy is still in place.

Mr. ROHRABACHER. So we changed the policy to make it more difficult for Egypt to obtain a weapons system.

Admiral RIXEY. We changed the policy.

Mr. ROHRABACHER. Okay. Let me just note that, Mr. Chairman, I hope we all are taking note that at a time when radical Islamists are murdering people all over the world, bombs are going off all over Egypt, I might say, which is on the front lines, we change the policy to make it more difficult for Egypt to have the weapons it needed in this struggle.

Let me ask you about Pakistan. I remember that a few years ago, when our brave military went in and took out Osama bin Laden, that there was a—that they had to go through all kinds of machinations on what type of equipment, where to go. They took a route to go get Osama bin Laden that was much more dangerous, because they were afraid that they might be shot down by the Pakistani Air Force for going into the airspace of Pakistan.

What kind of planes would they have been shot down by? Would they have been shot down by American airplanes?

Ambassador KAIDANOW. Sir, I mean, it is a little difficult for me to answer what is largely a hypothetical question.

I think what you are asking, though, is, you know, what kind of a discussion and what kind of relationship we have with Pakistan and ongoing. Is that what you are——

Mr. ROHRABACHER. I am alluding to the fact that we have our own military understanding that we can't trust them not to shoot down our own people, and we have ended up giving them modern weapon systems, and we continue to do so. Now, that is not your fault. You are running a system and being directed by political decisions.

But I would suggest, Mr. Chairman, that we need to go on the record here, on this part of our Government, to say that we are not going to be providing weapons to countries like Pakistan that we are afraid will shoot down our own people. And we know they are engaged in terrorism. We know what they have done now. They still hold Dr. Afridi, the man who helped us finger Osama bin Laden, the man who was responsible for slaughtering 3,000 Americans. They still hold him in a dungeon.

Mr. Chairman, we should be facilitating our support and our weapons systems to countries like Egypt that are fighting this threat to Western civilization, to all of civilization. And we should make it more difficult, not less difficult, for countries like Pakistan to get their hands on American weapons.

Thank you very much, Mr. Chairman.

Mr. POE. I thank the gentleman from California.

The Chair recognizes another member from California, the gentlelady, Mrs. Torres, for her questions.

Mrs. TORRES. Thank you so much, Mr. Chairman. Just 2 hours north of my colleague on the other side.

So thank you, both of you, for being here.

Ambassador Kaidanow, I want to go back to the question that you were answering earlier as it relates to Saudi Arabia.

So President Trump recently announced that we had reached a $110 billion arm deal with Saudi Arabia. Now, I know that there is some questions about, you know, is that really $110 billion? So we are not going to go through that today. But what are the conditions that you mention? What are those conditions that were placed on those weapons? You said that they—it was on Open Source. I have not seen it, so I would like some information.

Ambassador KAIDANOW. I think some of it has been reported in the press. In fact, I think this morning there was a piece on the issue.

I would not call them conditions, just to be clear. I want to sort of, again, give the understanding of—this is a dialogue that we have been having with the Saudi Government, and it is an important dialogue. I think they, themselves, recognize that some of the elements of their performance in Yemen have been problematic. They would like to improve those. We need to help them improve that performance.

The way, again, that we would hope to do that, one of the things that we recently notified to Congress is a $750 million training package for their air force. The idea behind that is very much to provide training on the law of armed conflict, to give them experience with targeting and vetting of targets, the kinds of things that, again, arguably, any military, but certainly in a combat situation, you would want to have them be more proficient at.

Mrs. TORRES. More proficient at targeting so they don't have so many civilian casualties?

Ambassador KAIDANOW. That's correct. Specifically to try and avoid civilian casualties. And that is important, you know, from our standpoint, from the U.S. Government standpoint, from theirs, I think, as well. And, increasingly, they acknowledge that.

So, again, I don't want to call it conditions. What I want to say is they have made commitments. I think those commitments are important. And the idea here is, again, to help them do some of that, because, in our view, it is better to engage and then to give them that assistance than it is to simply stand back and—because, you know, the situation in Yemen is very, very challenging. The Saudis face a number of threats on their border with Yemen. They also face a number of threats that emanate from the Houthis who, you know, clearly are being empowered by——

Mrs. TORRES. You also talked about monitoring and holding them accountable. So I want to ask you about the end-use monitoring. What is the process for making sure that arms don't end up in the wrong hands? Do you have the necessary resources, database, and the personnel to carry out effective end-use monitoring?

Ambassador KAIDANOW. Thank you for the question. The State Department has a program that it utilizes for end-use monitoring, but that is also amplified or supplemented by other programs at DOD and so forth. So it is not simply a function of what the State Department does.

We have a Blue Lantern program, it is called, that we utilize to ensure that there are ample checks, especially on the most sensitive weapon systems that we provide to some of our partners. We utilize some of our folks overseas in our Embassies to do some of those checking. Sometimes it is via the defense——

Mrs. TORRES. We have very limited time. Maybe we can follow up if there is some database——

Ambassador KAIDANOW. Absolutely.

Mrs. TORRES [continuing]. Somewhere were you have—you know, where those weapons have fallen into the wrong hands, what have you done to either get them back or destroy them.

Let's talk about Mexico. I have been very concerned about the illegal trafficking of the arms into Mexico. A lot of these arms are ending up in the wrong hands, gun traffickers and violent criminals, narcotraffickers. Given the widespread problems with corruption in Mexico, should we also be concerned about what is happening with guns that we sell into Mexico? How do we know we are selling to the right people?

Ambassador KAIDANOW. Well, again, and without getting into it too much here and offering up a specific briefing if you would like it on some of those issues. I think we do—we look very carefully at the end users who receive some of the weapons that we approve for sale.

Mrs. TORRES. Specifically, the corrupt police and military units.

Ambassador KAIDANOW. We look at the end-use recipients in any arms sale that we do, especially if it comes through the State Department. And, you know, there are some sales, obviously, that will eventually move again outside of our realm. But to the extent that it comes through because it is of a quality or a quantity that moves through the State Department for approval, we absolutely look to——

Mrs. TORRES. What happens when we find out, as in the state of Guerrero, that these weapons are ending up in the hands of narcotraffickers? What happens?

Ambassador KAIDANOW. Congresswoman, I would defer you probably to a more detailed briefing on all of the particularities of what we do with regard to Mexico, if that's all right. because I think there is a lot to talk about that.

Mrs. TORRES. I ran out of time, so thank you.

Ambassador KAIDANOW. Sure.

Mr. POE. I thank the gentlelady from California and for her line of questioning.

The Chair recognizes the gentleman from Pennsylvania, Mr. Perry.

Mr. PERRY. Thank you, Mr. Chairman.

Ambassador, Admiral, great to see you.

Ambassador, I want to continue the conversation that we had, I think it was last week, regarding the Saudi Arabian arms deal and the other side of the ledger, so to speak. So it might be a little bit off topic, but I think it is instructional.

So the context is that I am concerned about how much the export of Wahhabism was part of the deal, as you will recall. And so just to set the context, by 2013, 75 percent of North American Islamic centers relied on Wahhabi preachers who promote anti-Western ideas in person and online through sermons and through Saudi-produced literature. We think, since 1979, Saudi Arabia has engaged in a fairly persistent campaign of exporting that ideology throughout the world, spending about $4 billion annually on mosque, madrassas, preachers, students, and textbooks. I am interested in their sincerity, I guess, and how we monitor—what our metrics are in monitoring their efficacy adhering to their commitments. And so to further set the context, despite assurances that it would reform its educational curriculum by 2008—so this goes back nearly a decade. Let me just read some excerpts of current textbooks.

A 12th grade textbook professes that treachery, betrayal, and the denunciation of covenants are among the attributes of Jews. An 11th grade textbook teaches that cosmopolitan universities in the Middle East, such as the American universities in Beirut and Cairo, are examples of a modern-day crusade by Christians against Islam. And a 10th grade textbook on jurisprudence suggests that the most important debate about homosexuals is how best to execute them, whereas ISIS itself has used these textbooks issued by Saudi Arabia, their ministry of education, in its schools that it controls in Iraq and Syria.

To the best of your ability, in this setting, can you tell me who in the department—is there one person or is there a portion of the department, is there a crew that is going to monitor the efficacy of their pledge, so to speak? I understand, in talking to the Secretary yesterday, that they have pledged to change the textbooks and supply their organizations with those textbooks and also pull back current textbooks. That is what I understand, right, in this new global center for combating extremist ideology.

But I want to know, because we have been promised before, and we are tired of helping this sometimes ally when they don't seem to be really doing things in what is the United States's best interest, and if we are going to sell them things that they want and that we want them to have, they don't want to uphold their end of the deal. But, unfortunately, while I love the Reagan doctrine of trust but verify, in this instance, I prefer verify and then trust.

So what can you tell me about who is going to be monitoring that and how we are going to gauge their efficacy and what the penalties are for failure?

Ambassador KAIDANOW. Sir, thanks for the question. I will say that, in the first instance—and, of course, these issues that you have mentioned I think are of concern to us just like they are of concern to you. But I will tell you that, you know, in almost every instance, the people on the ground that we have there are the ones that are the closest to this, and they are the ones that monitor it. So our folks in our Embassy there are the ones that are responsible for looking at, you know, whether the Saudis live up to the commitments, again, the promises that they have made.

With regard to, you know, the State Department at large, we have a Bureau of Eurasian Affairs that, you know, again, concerns itself with these issues specifically. We also have public affairs people who look at this and the whole question of the promulgation of extremism through social media, through other means. These are the kinds of things that we preoccupy ourselves.

Mr. PERRY. Do we literally have someone in Saudi Arabia that is going to be at the receiving dock checking in X amount or tons or skids, pallets, what have you, of old textbooks to prove that they either came back, or do we have someone in the United States that is working with the Department of State to visit these places where the textbooks were issued to see the new ones come and the old ones go? Are we taking the Saudis' word for it? Because, apparently, we did since 2008. And you can see what we have gotten, which is very little. As a matter of fact, it has gone the other direction, in my opinion.

How are we verifying it specifically? And if you don't know and you got to get back to me later, I accept that. But I want to know the answer to that question.

Ambassador KAIDANOW. Understood, sir. And, no, I could not tell you sitting here, you know, whether we have an individual who is doing something like that. But I am happy to get back to you with an answer.

Mr. PERRY. All right. I think that we are all interested in that answer, and I think it is important to our national security in moving forward with this deal, as well within the answer, with the chairman's indulgence, the consequences to the adherence of this agreement for failure to live up to their commitment. Thank you.

Mr. POE. I thank the gentleman from Pennsylvania for his line of questioning.

Without objection, we have with us also Mr. Lieu from California, not a member of the subcommittee but a member of Foreign Affairs. The Chair will recognize him for 5 minutes.

Mr. LIEU. Thank you, Mr. Chairman, ranking member, for letting me participate in this hearing. And thank you, Ambassador Kaidanow and Admiral Rixey, for your public service.

We have had prior meetings on Saudi Arabia, so I would like to ask some questions for the record. As you know, the U.S. has been assisting Saudi Arabia in its war in Yemen. I don't have a problem with helping our ally Saudi Arabia, but many Members of Congress, on a bipartisan, bicameral basis, do have a significant problem when the Saudi-led military coalition is committing war crimes in Yemen.

I served in active duty in the Air Force. I am aware that, in the fog of war, you can make mistakes. Maybe three, four, five errant air strikes. I get that. But we are talking about dozens and dozens and dozens of reports from Human Rights Watch, Amnesty International, the U.N. have documented over 70 unlawful air strikes by the Saudi-led coalition. And this is as of last year. Who knows what it has done since then. And these are air strikes nowhere near military targets.

It freaked out our State Department so much that last year our State Department's lawyers initiated a review to see if U.S. personnel or others would be liable for aiding and abetting war crimes. The State Department stopped a sale of precision-guided munitions. The State Department this year has reversed.

So I would like to know what conditions have changed from, basically, last November to now that caused that reversal.

Ambassador KAIDANOW. As you pointed out, Congressman, I think this has been an ongoing evaluation. In other words—and as I said at the outset of my testimony, it is always a balance between the national security interest that we face and our allies face as against other considerations, many of which you just laid out, I think, very coherently.

With respect to Saudi and the coalition-led effort in Yemen, I think, again, the Saudis themselves have recognized that some of the aspects of how they have pursued that campaign are problematic. I think over time, their awareness of that has grown. I think their willingness and their ability to address some of those issues has grown. We have seen that both in the commitments they are willing to make to us as well as, again, in their willingness to accept some of the assistance that we can provide in order to help them do the things that, arguably, would improve their performance.

Again, as I said, they need to fully, and they have, commit to following the laws of armed conflict. They need to improve their vetting process for targeting and doing the kinds of things that we all know that need to be done, especially those of us who have done this kind of work previously. They need to be much more careful with their rules of engagement. These are the kinds of things they have to do.

Mr. LIEU. Have the Saudis made those commitments to the United States in writing?

Ambassador KAIDANOW. They have made commitments to us that we—again, that we have outlined for you, and we will——

Mr. LIEU. Could you give the committee the commitments they have made?

Ambassador KAIDANOW. We can definitely walk you through those commitments, absolutely.

Mr. LIEU. Okay. Thank you.

I would like to now shift to Qatar. As you know, last week, the President of the United States, through a series of tweets, accused Qatar of funding terrorism. The President essentially supported the blockade of Qatar led by Saudi Arabia and other Gulf nations. I am also reading reports that the United States just agreed to sell Qatar $12 billion worth of weapons, airplanes.

Is that true that we are selling them $12 billion worth of fighter jets?

Ambassador KAIDANOW. The fighter jet sale has been an ongoing deliberation and consideration for quite a while. Yes, the contract has just been signed for the sale.

Mr. LIEU. And I don't mean to be facetious with this, but does the President know that?

Ambassador KAIDANOW. I believe so.

Mr. LIEU. Okay. How do you square that sale, what the President has been saying about Qatar, since you said arm sales are an element of foreign policy?

Ambassador KAIDANOW. Absolutely. Yeah. Again, this goes back to the consideration of the wider array of foreign policy issues as regards the Gulf more broadly. It is not simply a question of the things that we concern ourselves with with regard to the extremism and so forth. Qatar needs to do some more things. The President, Secretary has made that clear. And we have made that clear to the Qataris. By the same token, the Qataris and the Gulf countries, as a whole, face certain threats from Iran, from other sources, but primarily from Iran, that they need to address through means that we can assist them with. These fighter sales are designed to address those kinds of threats.

So I think you can easily, you know, understand why we have to do multiple things at the same time.

Mr. LIEU. So thank you. So I don't take a position on this, because I need to find out more about it, my only point is that it is really confusing to world leaders, the Members of Congress, when the Trump administration does two exactly opposite things. And it is my hope that, as the administration grows and learns, that the administration stops doing that.

And with that, I yield back.

Mr. POE. I thank the gentleman.

The Chair recognizes another gentleman from California, Colonel Cook, for 5 minutes.

Mr. COOK. Thank you very much, Mr. Chair.

Ambassador, it is good to see you again. You are spending far too much time here. This very, very complicated business that we are talking about. You know, I am a historian and, go back, you read about Roosevelt and Churchill and who they were supporting in World War II. Sometimes the lines between enemy and friend was very, very complicated, how you could support the Soviets, some of the things that they did under the Stalin regime, and yet we are saying how much—you can go on and on and on. And I think a lot of these things weigh into the equation. Who is your enemy this week and—very, very complicated.

I do want to talk about the NATO arena and the dependence of many of our allies, Eastern European, quite frankly, on Soviet style equipment, both armor and air, that we have not weaned them off—maybe that is a bad phrase. But because of parts, because of systems, they still have to go back to the new Russia for those things that they had for years. And until they become a total member of NATO, in terms of our military equipment and everything else, I think it diminishes their capability as a true ally.

And if you could address that question right now, because it doesn't seem like a big priority, and yet countries there, they have been with us and everything else. But we expect them to come to the fight, when and if the Russians come across, such as the Rand study that was envisioned.

Ambassador KAIDANOW. Right. Thank you, sir, for the question. I would, first of all, just reassert our deep commitment to our NATO partners, as well as to our partners that are not necessarily members of the NATO but who are allies of ours and friends that we work with extensively. And in a number of cases, we obviously provide either assistance to them, grant assistance sometimes in that form, or in other forms.

Intraoperability, as you have indicated, is a huge, big issue for us. I highlighted it as one of the factors, you know, that we take into consideration when we make these decisions. I can't emphasize enough how much work we do with a number of our European partners, both within NATO and outside NATO, to ensure, again, that what you are talking about precisely takes place, that their weapon systems are modernized, that they are interoperable with ours, and to the extent that, again, that we need to provide assistance for them to do it, that we give them that.

Mr. COOK. Yeah. I think sometimes when we criticize our NATO partners for not meeting their 2 percent, I think if we are going to put all this pressure on them, and the fact that we are going to come, you know, to their aid if they are attacked, I think we have got to have—NATO standards applies to foreign military sales, at least my perspective. Other countries, obviously Saudi

Arabia, some of the others, it gets dicey because of some of the political considerations. Egypt, I thought were a bit heavy-handed. I know that still talking about the Morsi government, and everything like that, and the change by el-Sisi. But, of course, they did the same thing. They went right back to buying Russian military equipment because of what happened.

And I think, as you rightly pointed out, we have to take that variable into consideration. And we can argue all day about Saudi Arabia and Egypt and everything else. But NATO, we cannot criticize them. If they are having a tough time meeting the 2 percent, then we are not going to ensure that we do something to make sure that that is streamlined.

Admiral, would you comment on the short time I have left?

Admiral RIXEY. Well, we will honor any letter of request for capability. So I am seeing on my travels a desire to move away from Russian equipment and into NATO standard-type equipment. So we are prepared to execute if requested.

Mr. COOK. Okay. I yield back. Thank you.

Mr. POE. I thank the gentleman from California, Colonel Cook.

The Chair recognizes the gentleman from Virginia, Mr. Garrett, for his questions.

Mr. GARRETT. Thank you, Mr. Chairman, and thank the members of the panel for being here.

Generally, Mr. Chairman, when I ask a series of questions, there is an answer that I am driving at; that is not case today.

Understanding the importance of what you all do, of what FMS does, and what the DSCA does, our office publicly stated a policy that we think that this Nation should adhere to very early after being elected, and that is first to seek peace and stability in the world and, second, not to arm people who might later find themselves using those weapons against the United States or our allies.

There are literally dozens and dozens of nations, if you cover the gamut from main battle tanks to small arms, to whom we supply arms. And I don't necessarily object to that on its face. In fact, I think, in many instances, it is important to do. But I would ask you both—and this is a tough question—if you were forced to sort of predict a horrible worst-case scenario where U.S. weaponry was turned on U.S. forces or our allies, in what nation that we currently sell weapons to might that occur?

Because the answer can't be, oh, it could never happen. I will tell you—and I know I am burning my own time here. I grew up watching terror movements, watching government upheaval where the foreign fighters were armed with Soviet-Style weaponry. And it has galled me for the last decade as we see ISIS and AQAP and other elements in Humvees like the one I drove in, with rifles like the one I carried, firing weapon systems like the ones that our soldiers operate. It strikes me as a bad outcome.

So where might we see that again? And then I will give you a redemption clause, and how might we avoid that?

Ambassador KAIDANOW. I think it is a really important question, frankly. And I also think that it is, you know, a highly sensitive question. In other words, you know, how do you gauge that? You are asking, you know, a very difficult question to kind of get at.

I would say, at least when I think about it, and given the time that I have been doing this job, I worry perhaps a little bit less about some of the existing technology and what we have already provided. What I think about is the cutting-edge technology. The things that arguably, anyway, we have to be super careful about when we provide to other nations. And these are really open questions. I mean, we have to sit there and really think about, do we provide certain kinds of technology to certain partners, given some of our concerns, given the question as to whether those technologies will be adequately protected? And we don't take that lightly. I can just tell you——

Mr. GARRETT. I am going to interrupt, and I am not doing it to be rude.

Ambassador KAIDANOW. No, no.

Mr. GARRETT. It is a real hard question, given the professional nature of your individual responsibilities. And I don't want to get anybody in trouble here.

There are two ways this could happen, and maybe this will help you. It could happen because the nation state to whom we sold the weapons turns on us. Or it could happen, as it did in Iraq, because the nation state to whom we provided the weapons with the best of intentions abandoned those weapons and they fell into the hands of people who sought to do us and our allies harm.

Ambassador KAIDANOW. Yes.

Mr. GARRETT. Where might that be a possibility?

Ambassador KAIDANOW. I mean, you have highlighted places where, you know, in theory, that is possible. And there are places across the globe where we have, again, provided things, and you cannot always predict what will happen with regard to a government's stability or whether, you know, the next government will somehow find it in their interest, you know, to somehow do something against our interest.

But, again, I worry a little bit less about that with respect to the things already provided. I am now looking forward at the question of, you know, emerging technologies, how do we control for some of that in a very important environment in which we want American companies to have the ability to sell, and yet we also want to protect those technologies and not have them turned against our own forces. These are salient questions.

Mr. GARRETT. Admiral Rixey?

Admiral RIXEY. Well, I certainly don't want to speculate in this open forum. So if you will allow me, I will take that back to the Pentagon and get you a classified brief or something of that nature.

Mr. GARRETT. I would be delighted. I anticipate that you will proactively reach out to my office. I look forward to it. Thank you. I would yield back.

Mr. POE. I thank the gentleman.

The Chair recognizes the gentleman from New York, Mr. Zeldin.

Mr. ZELDIN. Well, thank you, Mr. Chair, and thank you to both of our witnesses for being here.

Ambassador, just for way of background, how long have you been in your current position, just so I know?

Ambassador KAIDANOW. I have been in the principal deputy slot since February of last year. So February 2016.

Mr. ZELDIN. Okay. And what were you doing just before that?

Ambassador KAIDANOW. I was the State Department coordinator for counterterrorism.

Mr. ZELDIN. Okay. Were you involved in all—because I just have some questions about the FMS-related transaction between the United States and Iran. Were you involved in that?

Ambassador KAIDANOW. No.

Mr. ZELDIN. Would you be able to answer any questions about that?

Ambassador KAIDANOW. Probably not in this setting.

Mr. ZELDIN. Well, let me try.

Ambassador KAIDANOW. Sure.

Mr. ZELDIN. When was the United States' claim against Iran—our claims against Iran—I am sorry.

When did the United States stop disputing our claims against Iran?

Ambassador KAIDANOW. Again, sir, just because this—I think this addresses a broader set of issues than I am necessarily responsible for in my portfolio at the State Department. I would offer, again, a briefing, if you would like it, on those specific issues.

Mr. ZELDIN. Okay. For decades, the United States was disputing that we owed Iran money for the sale. Do you know when we stopped disputing whether we owed that money?

Ambassador KAIDANOW. Sir, I don't have the history of all that in front of me right this minute. So, no, I would prefer to get back to you on the specifics.

Mr. ZELDIN. Okay. Do you know why we paid in cash?

Ambassador KAIDANOW. Again, this goes a little bit beyond my portfolio, so I really would prefer to give you a more detailed answer.

Mr. ZELDIN. You would be able to answer these questions, though, in another setting?

Ambassador KAIDANOW. We will, obviously, provide you any information we can.

Mr. ZELDIN. And you would be able to bring someone to that setting who would be able to answer what you might not be able to answer?

Ambassador KAIDANOW. We will do that.

Mr. ZELDIN. Do you know why the payment was made at the same time as the release of the American hostages?

Ambassador KAIDANOW. Sir, I can't answer, I think, any differently than I already have.

Mr. ZELDIN. All right. Just, I guess, procedurally, is there anything the way we handled this entire exchange over the course of decades that you think the United States can learn a lesson and handle it better going forward?

Ambassador KAIDANOW. Again, given the fact that, you know, we are not addressing in great detail the way that the issues unfolded, I think it would be probably better to discuss that in a briefing.

Mr. ZELDIN. There was a lot of concern here in Congress over, you know, many aspects of that exchange, historically speaking. When it happened, Iran was—they were canceling orders, and we ended up—the United States had parts that we were in the process of putting together. Iran takes over our Embassy. And everything that happens there at that point in time, you can make an argument of whether or not we would have owed them anything then.

But then there are these disputes, over the course of the years ahead, to be settled out in court or out of court, both the United States against Iran and Iran against the United States. And we were disputing whether or not we had owed this money to Iran. Yet what appears to me as a Member of Congress, and I know for many of my colleagues and for much of the American public, it seemed a bit odd that a position that the United States had for decades, that out of nowhere, we see the United States making a payment for the full principal amount, a generous interest amount, and it had to be delivered on a cash pallet to the Iranians at the same exact time as the Iranians releasing American prisoners. And it was the position of the administration that that was a coincidence and that one thing had absolutely nothing to do with the other. And I would be really interested in getting filled in on, if there is another, you know, 99 percent of the story that we are not familiar with, I would loved to be briefed up on it.

But without that information, I find it incredibly hard to believe that that was anything other than a ransom payment. And I find it hard to believe that I would be able to take the position that it was a coincidence. But also as it relates to, you know, our policies—lessons learned, our policies going forward—I don't know whether or not we even had owed the money. And that was a whole other dispute that was consistent—I say my position was consistent with U.S. position for decades.

So I certainly would appreciate that, Chairman, if we would have that opportunity to fill in the gaps that still exist.

I yield back.

Mr. POE. I appreciate the questions from the gentleman from New York and the gentleman from Virginia. I intend to figure out a way that we can have a classified briefing from you all on the issues raised by the gentleman from New York and Virginia and the gentleman from California as well.

I recognize myself for a line of questions.

We are all aware of the Turkish security detail that assaulted peaceful protesters on American soil and tried to prevent them from exercising constitutional rights of the right to assemble and to free speech. And I am still mad about that. I think other Members of Congress are as well.

The U.S. has a plan to sell small arms to security details like the Turkish goons that assaulted Americans. The chairman has written a letter to Secretary Tillerson asking to stop that sale until this is resolved about the assault. Where are we on that, Ambassador?

Ambassador KAIDANOW. Sir, thank you for the question. I think you have expressed concerns. We have some similar concerns that we expressed directly to our Turkish friends and colleagues. But this sale is one that obviously is going to have to be looked at and reviewed. It is still in the process of review, given the fact that now the law enforcement process is in play. Rather than sort of give you an end state, I would like to just come back to you soon and give you an update on where we are with it. But it is still in review. It has not——

Mr. POE. You understand, as oversight on this issue, members of the Foreign Affairs Committee, through the chairman, have said suspend those sales till this is resolved and the folks that committed these crimes against Americans on American soil is resolved. I think that is atrocious that that would ever occur. So that is our position. And we hope that you will suspend those sales until this is done.

This whole concept of sales to foreign countries, hopefully folks that are friendly to us, is complicated, because the idea that if we don't sell to country X, then they are going to go buy from the Russians, the Chinese, whoever they can get these weapon systems from. It is a political issue, but it is also a security issue for the U.S. to have partners that look to us rather than look to the Russians or the Chinese. I understand that.

Let's talk about Lebanon. We are in the process of selling weapons to Lebanon. Reports are the Lebanese Government gives those small arms to Hezbollah, a terrorist group. Where are we on that? How do we know that Lebanon—those arms don't end up in the possession of Hezbollah, a terrorist group in Lebanon and now in other countries as well?

Ambassador or Admiral, either one of you. How do we know that is not going to happen?

Ambassador KAIDANOW. Thank you again for the question. So we are very resolute in supporting the Lebanese armed forces. Those armed forces we regard as the most important guarantor, if you will, of Lebanese sovereigty and the ability of Lebanon as a country to maintain its integrity. We consider that very important with regard to what is going on in the region now, given the threat of ISIS or Daesh, given the threat of Iran extending its arc of influence through——

Mr. POE. I get that. How do we know they don't end up in the possession of Hezbollah?

Ambassador KAIDANOW. We are watching very, very carefully. Extremely carefully. And we are confident, thus far, that no weapons have been transferred from the Lebanese Government or the Lebanese armed forces into the hands of those who should not get it, including Hezbollah.

Mr. POE. Do you have a comment, Admiral?

Admiral RIXEY. Well, sir, we would, of course, execute our Golden Sentry program and end-use monitoring in that country to ensure that that does not happen.

Mr. POE. I want to turn to Pakistan. We have been having the issue with Pakistan whether they are loyal or playing us for years on the issue of aid to Pakistan and sales to Pakistan. As mentioned by the gentleman from California, Mr. Rohrabacher, when we went in to get Osama bin Laden, we were concerned about the Pakistanis scrambling F-16s that we made and sold to the Pakistanis so that they wouldn't shoot down Americans who were doing the job of taking out this terrorist.

I personally think Pakistan plays the United States, because they turn to China if we don't help them. I understand all that. They have nuclear weapons, and we want to have a relationship with them so that they don't look to China. I get all that. But are we doing anything different on sales to Pakistan to make sure those sales of whatever it is aren't used against us directly or used against us indirectly because of the military helping the Taliban in Afghanistan where we have our troops, and those weapons could be used against the United States? Are we doing anything different to make sure that doesn't happen or are we still using the same formula?

Ambassador KAIDANOW. No. I mean, I think what we applied to Pakistan is what we applied to a number of our partner countries. But with Pakistan, we have a robust end-use monitoring program, extremely robust, to ensure that the items that we provide for them are used appropriately and within the boundaries of what we have asked them to accomplish.

We, as you say, regard Pakistan as an important partner on counterterrorism issues. They will be essential in bringing the Afghan Taliban to the table for peace talks. There are a number of things where we need their cooperation and their assistance. And we do want to help them on the counterterrorism front. But on the other hand, again, we have very big concerns that we continuously front with them on support for Haqqani, on support for other things. This has been made clear to the Pakistani Government at the highest level.

Mr. POE. Admiral, you don't want to comment?

Admiral RIXEY. I defer to State.

Mr. POE. All right. I am out of time.

I will mention to the subcommittee and to the witnesses, I appreciate you all being here. We will figure out a way to have a classified briefing, because we have gone about halfway on the questions that we are asking. Many Members of Congress want a bottom-line answer to the questions that they ask about the different countries during their questioning here in open forum. So we will work on that.

I thank both of you for being here. I know you all have time constraints. I was just making sure there is not anybody else here.

The subcommittee is adjourned. Thank you very much. I thank the members for being here.

[Whereupon, at 11:32 a.m., the subcommittee was adjourned.]

A P P E N D I X

SUBCOMMITTEE HEARING NOTICE
COMMITTEE ON FOREIGN AFFAIRS
U.S. HOUSE OF REPRESENTATIVES
WASHINGTON, DC 20515-6128

Subcommittee on Terrorism, Nonproliferation, and Trade
Ted Poe (R-TX), Chairman

TO: MEMBERS OF THE COMMITTEE ON FOREIGN AFFAIRS

You are respectfully requested to attend an OPEN hearing of the Committee on Foreign Affairs, to be held by the Subcommittee on Terrorism, Nonproliferation, and Trade in Room 2172 of the Rayburn House Office Building (and available live on the Committee website at http://www.ForeignAffairs.house.gov):

DATE: Thursday, June 15, 2017

TIME: 10:00 a.m.

SUBJECT: Foreign Military Sales: Process and Policy

WITNESSES: The Honorable Tina S. Kaidanow
                   Acting Assistant Secretary
                   Bureau of Political-Military Affairs
                   U.S. Department of State

                   Vice Admiral Joseph Rixey
                   Director
                   U.S. Defense Security Cooperation Agency

By Direction of the Chairman

53

COMMITTEE ON FOREIGN AFFAIRS

MINUTES OF SUBCOMMITTEE ON ______*Terrorism, Nonproliferation, and Trade*______ HEARING

Day___*Thursday*___ Date___*June 15, 2017*___ Room_____*2172*_____

Starting Time ___*10:22 a.m.*___ Ending Time ___*11:31 a.m.*___

Recesses |____| (____to____) (____to____) (____to____) (____to____) (____to____) (____to____)

Presiding Member(s)
Chairman Ted Poe

Check all of the following that apply:

Open Session ☑   Electronically Recorded (taped) ☑
Executive (closed) Session ☐   Stenographic Record ☑
Televised ☑

TITLE OF HEARING:

"Foreign Military Sales: Process and Policy"

SUBCOMMITTEE MEMBERS PRESENT:

Reps. Poe, Keating, Cook, Torres, Perry, Zeldin, Mast, Garrett

NON-SUBCOMMITTEE MEMBERS PRESENT: *(Mark with an * if they are not members of full committee.)*

Rohrabacher, Lieu

HEARING WITNESSES: Same as meeting notice attached? Yes ☑ No ☐
(If "no", please list below and include title, agency, department, or organization.)

STATEMENTS FOR THE RECORD: *(List any statements submitted for the record.)*

SFRs submitted by Reps. Ted Poe and William Keating

TIME SCHEDULED TO RECONVENE __________
or
TIME ADJOURNED ___*3:19 p.m.*___

Subcommittee Staff Associate

9 781973 947578